CATCH·THEM THINKING·IN SCIENCE

A Handbook of Classroom Strategies

Sally Berman

IRI/Skylight Publishing, Inc.
Palatine, Illinois

Catch Them Thinking in Science: A Handbook of Classroom Strategies

IRI/Skylight Publishing, Inc.,
2626 S. Clearbrook Dr., Arlington Heights, IL 60005-5310
800-348-4474, 847-290-6600
Fax 847-290-6609
info@iriskylight.Com
http://www.iriskylight.com

Editing: Erica Pochis, Janet Culloton, Julia E. Noblitt, Robin Fogarty
Type Composition: Donna Ramirez
Graphics: David Stockman and Michael A. Melasi
Book Design: Michael A. Melasi

Library of Congress Card Catalog Number 93-78421

Printed in the United States of America.

ISBN 0-932935-55-9

0782C-8-98CHG
Item Number 1103

06 05 04 03 02 01 00 99 98   15 14 13 12 11 10 9 8 7 6 5 4 3

Table of Contents

PART I: CATCH THEM GATHERING INFORMATION

PART II: CATCH THEM PROCESSING INFORMATION

PART III: CATCH THEM ANALYZING AND APPLYING INFORMATION

Acknowledgments

The whole thing started because of the kids—those wonderful, amazing, frustrating, challenging, warm, exciting students with whom I work one hundred eighty-five days every year. I needed to know that we were speaking the same language and that they were puzzling out answers to problems and making connections with prior content knowledge in science and with life outside of the science classroom. I wanted to focus their efforts on developing teamwork and thoughtfulness. I looked around for materials that contained cooperative/cognitive activities in science. None existed. I needed to invent my own student-centered lessons or go back to doing things the teacher-centered way. The latter was unthinkable. The students deserved better. The students of Palatine High School provided the primary motivation for writing this book.

It must have been serendipity. When I was about one-fourth of the way through the project, I mentioned to Jim Bellanca and Robin Fogarty that I was writing a book of activities for students to use in my classroom. Jim said, "Bring it to us—we'll publish it." Robin said, "We're really looking for a *Catch Them Thinking in Science*. Will you write it for us?" What began as a very chemistry-specific work evolved into a book that included sample lessons in all science disciplines. Robin's question gave me the courage to step outside of my specific content area and expand my horizons, and Jim and Robin's encouragement kept me going.

Fellow Palatine High School science teachers Ed Richardson, Floyd Rogers, Kathy Seilheimer, Sue Anderson, and Tony Krotz loaned me biology, earth science, and physical science books which provided content ideas for some of the lessons. Gary

Kraft's need to teach his students to organize information in Venn diagrams led to the frontload activity for "Frogs and Salamanders." Roy Schodtler served as sounding board and devil's advocate. His valuable questions guided the revision of several lessons. Jim Tefft took the time to explain some basic physics to me until I could not help but understand it—which is quite an accomplishment. Ken Spengler, department chairman, mentor, good friend, and chemistry buddy, has given me ideas and inspiration for as long as we have taught together—which is almost thirty years. He developed the prototype of the "Letter to Uncle Chester" from a suggestion that we heard at a Chemistry West meeting. Bob Zuidema, a Palatine High School physics teacher of almost fifteen years ago, planted the seeds for "Hide in Plain Sight" before he left us. Those seeds may have taken a long time to germinate, but they popped up right when I needed them most. Mike Offutt of Barrington High School confirmed my belief in storyboarding. Mike's students draw comic strips which are very much the same thing. Buddy Hughes, commercial artist and former Palatine High School student and baseball pitcher actually introduced me to storyboarding as it is used in advertising in the late 1970s. I did not see the use then, but storyboards have become one of my favorite cooperative, cognitive activities. Lee Marek, DeWayne Lieneman, Bob Lewis, and other Chemistry West regulars have encouraged the humorous twist found in some of the lessons in this book. I can never thank them enough for sharing so many of their own lessons and ideas over the years. Some strategies, like the black boxes in "Mental Modeling" have been around for so long, in so many different forms, that I do not really know where or when they were first invented—and I cannot find anyone else who knows either.

On those long evenings when I knew that I had to write (because of that contract that I signed in a weak moment), but I really did not feel like it, Murphy, the Siberian Husky who refused to grow up, gave me companionship by bringing her rawhide chew into the office with me and gnawing on it while I typed. When she got tired of that, she gently rested her chin on my toes and went to sleep. She and her pal Medved also let me know when it was time to quit for the night by staging their version of "Duel of the Titans" on my feet and all around my chair. They would growl and lunge at each other taking care that I was in the way of the countercharge. Just try to keep typing with one hundred pounds of dogs knocking your chair around the room. "Knock it off!" I would yell. They would quit for an instant, grin at me, and start up all over again. I would quit in self-defense.

My husband, Al, endured being a writing widower nights, weekends, and during our vacations from school. He found ways to keep himself amused while I typed (or sat and stared at the wall asking myself, "Where am I going with this one?"). He was and is my rock, my best friend, my champion, my knight in shining armor. He brought me coffee, aspirin, and love, took messages, ran errands, absorbed my frustrations, picked up Chinese food, bought groceries, called off the dogs, encouraged me when the going got rough, proofread copy, bought me flowers, and kept me believing that I could finish this project.

Thank you everyone who helped and encouraged me, and thank you, kids. This book would not have been imagined had it not been for you.

Foreword

Teachers everywhere are enrolling in workshops and courses devoted to teaching higher-level thinking skills. Of necessity, most of these are generic in nature, offered for teachers in all areas and often all grade levels as well. Translating these new ideas into lesson plans takes time that busy science teachers may not have. In addition, the nature of scientific thinking presents its own special opportunities and challenges.

Sally Berman has assembled a collection of tested techniques that work with real students in real classrooms. The strategies in this book can serve as templates that will transform traditional science topics into exercises that engage young minds. Memorizing content will be replaced by thoughtful effort that forges mental connections and sticks to the educational ribs. This book blends sound educational theory with practical, worthwhile activities that students enjoy.

Kenneth Spengler
Science Department Chairman
Palatine High School
Palatine, Illinois
April 1993

Introduction:
Catch Your Students Thinking in Science

You have probably been wondering how to design units of study in science that encourage your students to become better thinkers. The organization of this book is designed to help you do just that. We science teachers proclaim that we want to help our students develop their thinking skills, but we very often try to build those skills without following a blueprint. We may get lucky, but we may also leave less gifted students feeling baffled, frustrated, and confused.

Part I
Part I of this book describes and gives some examples of activities that are useful to students who are gathering information. Useful higher-level thinking must begin here. Students cannot process what they do not have. The activities help hook student interest, facilitate their learning, and make them responsible for doing the work that you want them to do. As students do these activities, they will make their thinking visible by using grids for organizing information. They will also be asked to begin keeping a class log or journal, so they will need to have notebooks in which they can keep their logs or journals organized. You may have them use whatever type of notebook you prefer. I like three-ring binders; they allow students to insert artifacts that are related to the log or journal entries. Part I includes an activity that introduces students to think-pair-share—a powerful technique for gathering answers to questions that students may not have used before. It encourages students to become more reflective and less impulsive by asking them to wait until called on before telling you (and the rest of the class) their answers to questions. Stress the idea that by decreasing their impulsive urges to blurt out answers, students allow the whole class to gather better information.

Part II

Part II includes activities that can be used to process information. This is where the fun really begins! Students are asked to analyze, visualize, organize, and explain information in a variety of ways. Cooperative learning enhances this phase of their learning. Be sure that your students understand the skills that make cooperative groups function effectively and the roles that members of cooperative groups are asked to perform. You can find a thorough explanation of cooperative group skills and roles in *Blueprints for Thinking in the Cooperative Classroom* (Bellanca and Fogarty, 1991, IRI/Skylight). Individuals may be asked to do a rough draft of many of the assigned activities to share with teammates in class. When the teams get together, everyone benefits from the exchange of ideas.

Students will use a variety of graphic organizers to make their thinking visible as they do the activities. They will use webs, Venn diagrams, fishbones, matrices (grids), and they will be asked to take good notes (be good information gatherers) as they carry out their assigned cooperative roles. Several of the activities involve brainstorming. You may want to remind students of the DOVE guidelines (Bellanca and Fogarty, 1991) before they begin these activities. There is a DOVE guidelines blackline master at the back of this book that makes an excellent transparency for the overhead projector (see page 94).

Part III

Part III describes activities that can be used to analyze and apply information. Look at the products of these activities as alternatives to traditional assessment tools. The best products again come from cooperative learning teams. Students are asked to design products that combine verbal, visual, and analytical skills. Their visible thinking appears in mind maps, storyboards and other graphics, and right-angle thinking diagrams. This part stresses writing skills. They may complain that the activities are hard, but they will come away from them with a better understanding of the topic than you may have believed possible.

Processing

Looking back and reflecting cognitively and metacognitively on what has been done, what has been learned, and what aspects of the activity can be transferred to new situations is a key component of all of the activities in all three parts. Often this involves having all groups present their products, applications, or ideas for transfer to the rest of the class. This sharing is called a wraparound. You may have teams draw numbers to decide who presents first, who presents second, and so on during the wraparound, or you may ask the class if teams would like to volunteer to decide who answers first, who answers second, and so forth. It is important to make the order of presentation strictly random by asking for volunteers or handing out numbers. Students who perceive that you are calling on them because you believe that they are less skilled or less prepared than others and you want to teach them a lesson are unlikely to become productively involved in the activities. I find that a good preparation for metacognitive wraparounds is asking students to write in their logs, using Mrs. Potter's Questions (Bellanca and Fogarty, 1991) as the cue for the log entry. (See page 95 for a blackline master.)

Mrs. Potter's Questions ask:
What were we supposed to do?
What did we do well?
What would we do differently next time?
How do we see an expert helping us improve?

I like to add one more question: How can we use the strategies we learned or the information that we gained outside of this specific activity? Individual students write the answers in their logs. Students may discuss their thoughts with their teammates or pair and share. You can then draw names out of a hat or ask for volunteers to share their ideas with the rest of the class. The more you share information and ideas, the more valuable the lessons become.

One word of caution. It takes time to do thinking skill activities and to monitor the use of these skills in the classroom. You must decide whether you want to take the time to do a good job, or whether short-term memorization and high scores on multiple choice tests satisfy you. Please consider, as you make your decision, that factual knowledge in science doubles every year. By the time your students finish their formal education and become independent adults, many of your facts will be outdated. Memorizers may be left behind. Thinkers will not be.

The strategies and activities that I have included in this book are ones that I find very effective with my students. I have used all of them in my classroom at one time or another. Do not let the variety overwhelm you. Pick one or two from each part to try, and then add others as you become more familiar with the first few. Get other teachers involved in using the strategies. Form a support team so that you can help each other. Fine tune your lessons as you try them, and celebrate success when it happens. Include your students in your celebrations. Catch them being good at thinking in science!

How to Use This Book

The chapters in *Catch Them Thinking in Science* have been grouped into three major parts:

I.   Catch Them Gathering Information

II. Catch Them Processing Information

III. Catch Them Analyzing and Applying Information

The chapters in **Catching Them Gathering Information** focus on collecting facts and organizing thoughts. The class log as a tool for collecting information and thoughts is first introduced in this part.

The chapters in **Catch Them Processing Information** stress organizing and making sense of information in a variety of ways. It is here that critical thinking mental muscles are exercised.

The chapters in **Catch Them Analyzing and Applying Information** feature activities that combine critical and creative thinking and transfer. Skills that are needed to successfully complete these lessons are imbedded in Part I and Part II lessons. Be sure that students have a firm foundation before jumping into a Part III lesson.

How the Chapters Are Organized

Each chapter in all three parts is organized into these sections:

1. **Background**: includes a brief theoretical basis for and/or rationale for the activity

2. **Thinking Skill(s)**: names the specific thinking mirco-skill(s) stressed in the activity

3. **Focus Activity**: describes the hook that is used to engage students in the lesson

4. **Objective(s)**: names the skill(s) that the lesson is intended to develop

5. **Input**: outlines the materials that the teacher needs and the frontload that the students need to do the lesson successfully

6. **Activity**: describes what the students and teacher will actually do during the lesson

7. **Cognitive Discussion**: tells how the students and teacher will process the content that has been learned by doing the lesson

8. **Metacognitive Discussion**: suggests questions that students can use to reflect on the effectiveness of the learning process and how the process can be applied to learn new content

9. **Closure**: provides a follow-up to the activity; it may be a new, related activity or it may be a sharing of the product of the activity

You may be able to use some lessons exactly as they appear. Others may focus on specific content that is not included in your science curriculum. Let them serve as models for your own lessons that do fit your curriculum. Once you have seen examples of "The People Search," for example, you can write your own. As you develop your lessons, let the organization of this book serve as a guide for developing your students' thinking skills.

This book's organization was inspired by Oliver Wendell Holmes, who said: "One-story intellects, two-story intellects, three-story intellects with skylights. All fact-collectors, who have no aim beyond their facts, are one-story men. Two-story men compare, reason, generalize, using the labors of the fact-collectors as well as their own. Three-story men idealize, imagine, predict; their best illumination comes from above, through the skylight." (Holmes, 1916)

How to Assess Your Students

One method of assessment, the log, is used throughout this book.

What Is the Log?

It is a record of a student's thoughts and learnings for your class. The log includes focus writing, "Think!" (from think-pair-share), items from cognitive and metacognitive processing, sketches, spontaneous entries, and maybe some class notes.

Why Ask Students to Keep a Log?

A log helps students keep track of much more than new content learning. I find it helpful to begin class by asking students to summarize what we did in class the day before and to express any thoughts that they feel may distract them from doing their best in class that day. At the beginning of a new topic, students may focus by writing down their impressions or thoughts about a key word (i.e., what do they think when they hear "element," "gene," "ocean").

As study of the topic proceeds, students are encouraged to jot down clarifications, corrections, and additions to their original impressions or thoughts. The log becomes a record of the progress they have made as they study the topic. At this point, it may include class notes, sketches, diagrams, lists of ideas from "Share" (think-pair-share), or personal goals for making progress in their understanding of the topic. They may write questions that they want to have answered. Encourage them to make their logs a record of their complete experience as they study the topic.

To that end, many of the cognitive and metacognitive discussions that are suggested for activities in this book involve writing or sketching log entries. As students write or draw, they clarify their thinking about the lesson. This helps them remember it better. End of class logging also provides for a quiet time for students to unwind and prepare for the next class or activity.

What Do You Do While They Log?

YOU LOG! Model the behavior that you want from them. They will perceive it as being worthwhile if they see you doing it too. The fastest way for you to discourage students' belief in logging is to neglect doing it yourself.

What Are the Benefits of Logging?

Students are more focused at the beginning of class. Because you ask them to summarize the previous lesson on the topic, they find it easier to connect information. They have a running record of the development of a topic, which is invaluable when time comes to review.

Students also have fun with their logs. Many of my students record personal feelings and thoughts that they find very amusing a few months later. The log becomes a diary as well as a record of class work and tool for reflection and improved thinking.

Is It Hard to Assess Student Logs?

Not really. Keep in mind that what you are looking for is an indication of clear expression, improved understanding, improved use of thinking skills, and honest reflection. You will soon find that you enjoy assessing logs much more than scantron tests. They give you the opportunity to witness students' growth and progress from their perspective.

The Three-Story Intellect

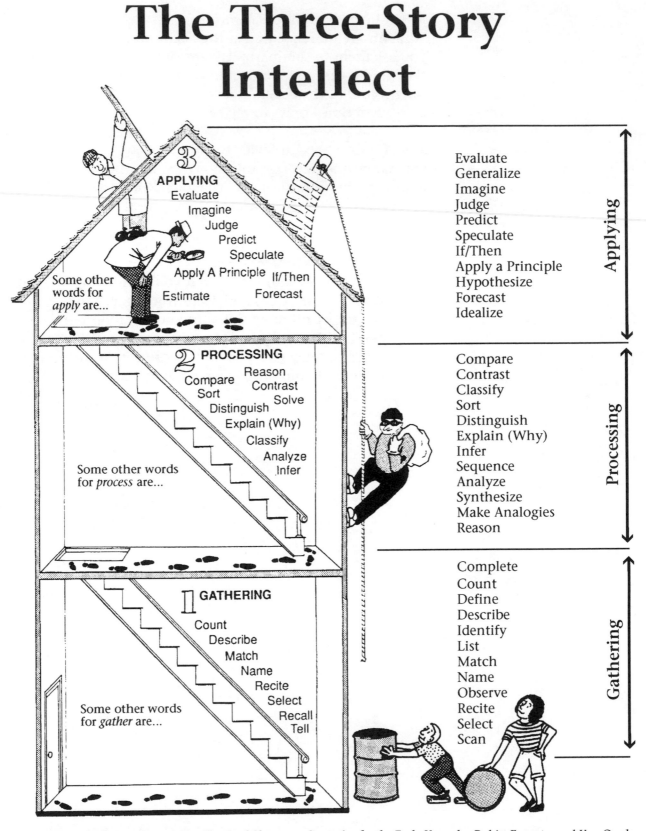

From *Start Them Thinking: A Handbook of Classroom Strategies for the Early Years,* by Robin Fogarty and Kay Opeka, ©1988 by IRI/Skylight Publishing, Inc.

Part I

Catch Them
GATHERING
Information

Chapter
1

Getting to Know You

The People Search

BACKGROUND

As students participate in a people search, they recall prior knowledge, explain or teach information to their classmates, listen to one another for understanding, use the vocabulary of the unit that they are about to study, and interact with one another, exchanging answers in a safe-risk climate.

THINKING SKILLS

Recalling, Investigating, Understanding

FOCUS ACTIVITY

Give or review the rules for doing a people search. Students must get out of their desks and move around the room. They must approach that classmate, use good eye contact, and use a classmate's name in asking a classmate to sign their people search sheets. They may even offer to sign a classmate's sheet. However, remind students that when they sign they signify their ability to answer that item. As they give and receive signatures, they learn the answers to the items on the people search. They must obtain the signature of a different classmate for each item on the people search. Set a time limit; one minute per item is a good rule of thumb.

OBJECTIVES

To transfer prior knowledge to the new unit of study and to communicate that knowledge to one's classmates; to begin using the vocabulary of the new unit of study and to obtain a glimpse of the content of the unit.

INPUT

Explain to the students how important it is to express themselves clearly and to check for understanding by having the student for whom they are signing repeat or paraphrase the answer. Encourage students to take notes on their people search sheets about answers that they may forget. Remind students that their signatures mean they have the answers to the items for which they sign and that they may be called on to give those answers during a class discussion which will follow the people search.

ACTIVITY

1. Distribute a copy of the people search to each student. (Two different people searches are provided on pages 6 and 7. Feel free to use the blackline master on page 96 to create your own people search.) Ask a student to review the instructions for doing the activity.

2. Signal when time is up and ask all students to please return to their seats.

COGNITIVE DISCUSSION

Go over the people search item by item. Encourage students to take notes during the discussion. Call on students at random to give the answers. Below is one effective calling-on strategy.

Call on a student, selected at random, and ask that student who signed his or her sheet for Item 1. Then ask the student who signed the sheet to give the answer. If the answer is incomplete or incorrect, ask for volunteers to add to the answer. Then call on a different student and ask that student who signed his or her sheet for Item 2. Again, the student who signed is asked to give the answer, and the class is asked to add to the answer if necessary. The teacher may also add to the answer if he or she wishes to clarify the answer or introduce additional information. The random questioning and answering continue until the last item on the people search is answered.

Another effective strategy is to call on a student, selected at random, and ask that student who signed his or her sheet. Then tell the student, "Explain or tell us his or her answer in your own words." Have volunteers add to the answer if it is incomplete or incorrect. Either strategy holds students accountable for signing only if they know or can explain the answer for an item on the people search.

METACOGNITIVE DISCUSSION	Tell the students to:

1. Write down at least two new things that they learned by doing the people search.

2. Explain why some cute items are included. A cute earth science item might be: Name three things that can rock.

3. Divide students into groups of three and have them make a list of all the new things learned by members of the group. Have them make a second list of reasons for inclusion of the cute people search items.

CLOSURE

On the blackboard, overhead projector, or newsprint, make an unduplicated web of the new learnings. Ask each group in turn to tell one new thing learned by a member of the group. Continue until the web includes all new learnings. Conclude by asking students to write a log entry that focuses on two new things they learned about the content and how they can use those things outside of class.

People Search: The Ground We Walk On

Directions: Find someone who can give you an answer for each of the items below. A classmate may sign for only one item, so you will need eleven different signatures. Sign only if you know the answer or be prepared to accept the consequences!

My signature means that I...

1. can identify the four most common elements in the earth's crust.

    _____

2. can predict where I would go in the United States to find an active volcano.

    _____

3. can describe the appearance of marble.

    _____

4. do not take good grades for granite!

    _____

5. can guess why a compass goes crazy in northeast Minnesota.

    _____

6. like rocking chairs.

    _____

7. can name three kinds of rock.

    _____

8. have used lava soap.

    _____

9. can explain what limestone and coal have in common.

    _____

10. can compare the properties of quartz and diamond.

    _____

11. am using a metamorphic rock to sign this paper.

    _____

People Search: Mirror, Mirror on the Wall...

Directions: Find someone who can give you an answer for each of the items below. A classmate may sign for only one item, so you will need ten different signatures. Sign only if you know the answer or be prepared to accept the consequences!

My signature means that I...

1. can name the process that produces an image when I look in a mirror.

   _____

2. can explain what is wrong with a mirror image.

   _____

3. can color inside the lines.

   _____

4. can describe why glass makes a good mirror and brick does not.

   _____

5. can define concave and convex.

   _____

6. like optical illusions.

   _____

7. can tell you what is different about reflections seen inside a spoon.

   _____

8. can explain why roses are red and violets are blue.

   _____

9. used a mirror this morning.

   _____

10. can complete the quotation used as the title of this activity.

   _____

KNL

What do we Know?
What do we Need to know?
What have we Learned?

Chapter 2

BACKGROUND

You may have seen this activity before. I have changed Want to know to Need to know because my students respond more responsibly to the latter. This is an activity that gets students hooked into a topic before formal discussion begins. It can also save you time. If they already have a lot of information about some aspects of the topic, you do not have to spend class time dispensing that information!

THINKING SKILLS

Recalling, Investigating, Predicting

FOCUS ACTIVITY

Set up a KNL grid on the board, overhead, or newsprint. There is a blackline master of the KNL grid on page 97. Newsprint makes it easier to save the grid for future use. Explain to the students that they will make their contributions to the "K" and "N" columns right away and that they will fill in the "L" column toward the end of the unit.

K (What do we Know?)	N (What do we Need to know?)	L (What have we Learned?)

OBJECTIVES

To recall prior knowledge about a topic; to use that information to predict what additional information may be needed for better understanding of the topic; to begin investigation of a topic.

INPUT	See focus activity.
ACTIVITY	Divide students into groups of three. Give the groups some time to list their Ks and Ns. Be sure that each group has a recorder who writes down the list as the group brainstorms. Call on groups for their Ks first. Ask each group for one item before any group contributes a second item. Keep going until all of the Ks for the class are recorded on the master grid (on newsprint, the overhead, or the board). Respond to contributions by saying "thank you" or by repeating the contribution as you record it. This is not the time to judge contributions. You may correct misunderstandings as you study the material. Repeat the process for Ns.
COGNITIVE DISCUSSION	At some future time—as you complete the unit—repeat the process for Ls. This is the time to go back to the original Ks and cross out any that are incorrect. Ask students to help you find them.
METACOGNITIVE DISCUSSION	Doing the sections of the grid will involve students in cognitive discussion of the material in their small groups and with the whole class. You may ask them to process metacognitively by recording new learnings and corrections of misconceptions in their logs. You may also encourage them to complete logging stems like the following: I could have used the KNL process when... I will be able to use the KNL process when... I am still confused about...
CLOSURE	Ask students to combine the corrected Ks and the Ls into a master list of information about the topic. Tell them that they may organize the information as an outline, map, concept web, or in other ways that will make it useful to them. Tell them to integrate the two lists rather than simply tacking the Ls after the corrected Ks. Have the small groups of students present their outline, map, or concept web to the class as a review of the topic.

Chapter 3

What I Really Do Not Understand Is...

Asking Questions

BACKGROUND	The progress of science depends on the quality and quantity of questions that scientists working in real-life laboratories ask. Students need to be taught that some questions are minnow questions (also known as skinny questions)—questions that ask for quick recall of facts and can be answered quickly. Other questions are whale questions (also known as fat questions)—questions that ask for analysis or explanation of facts or that ask for predictions based on prior knowledge. Students need to realize that the kinds of questions that they ask determine the answers they will get and that asking the right questions will help them in many different situations.
THINKING SKILL	Investigating
FOCUS ACTIVITY	To demonstrate the difference between minnow questions and whale questions, ask the students: What natural disaster disrupted the 1989 World Series in San Francisco?
	One of them will know the right answer: an earthquake.
	Then ask them: Predict the changes that might have occurred in the life of your family if you had been living in San Francisco during the 1989 World Series.
	Stress the idea that answering a whale question completely involves asking yourself a lot of follow-up minnow questions. Give some examples—what might have happened to our

electricity? our telephone? our gas lines? the streets we take to school or to work? the newspaper delivery? the grocery store? The list goes on and on.

OBJECTIVES

To identify questions as whale questions or minnow questions; to write questions about the science unit prior to studying the content.

INPUT

Do an introductory people search for the unit like the ones on pages 6 and 7.

Give students the Minnows and Whales graphic and the Asking Questions graphic (see pages 14 and 15).

ACTIVITY

1. Tell students to individually write at least three questions about the upcoming unit. Suggest that reviewing the notes that they made during the people search may help them ask the right questions. Encourage students to write whale questions. (Writing the individual questions may be assigned as homework.)

2. Divide students into groups of three. Have each group make a list of all the different questions asked by members of the group. Tell students to file the lists in their notebooks for future reference.

3. At the end of the unit of study, tell students to get out their lists of questions. Tell them that it is now time to answer the questions and decide which were whales and which were minnows.

4. Have each group pass a copy of its questions to another group.

5. Tell the groups of students to answer the questions from the list that they received. Give the groups fifteen minutes to write their answers to the questions.

6. When time is up, ask the groups to pass the questions and answers back to the group that wrote the questions.

COGNITIVE DISCUSSION	On the blackboard, overhead projector, or newsprint, write a list of all the different questions asked by groups in the class. Call on groups in turn to contribute one question to the list. Continue until all questions are listed. Encourage students to copy this list of questions. Tell the students that this list of questions will be a review sheet for the unit. Give the students time to work in their groups to answer the questions.
METACOGNITIVE DISCUSSION	Tell the groups to label their questions as whales or minnows and to explain their labels.
CLOSURE	Ask students to write a log entry that describes how teachers use whale and minnow questions during class discussions or when they create worksheets and tests.

Minnows and Whales

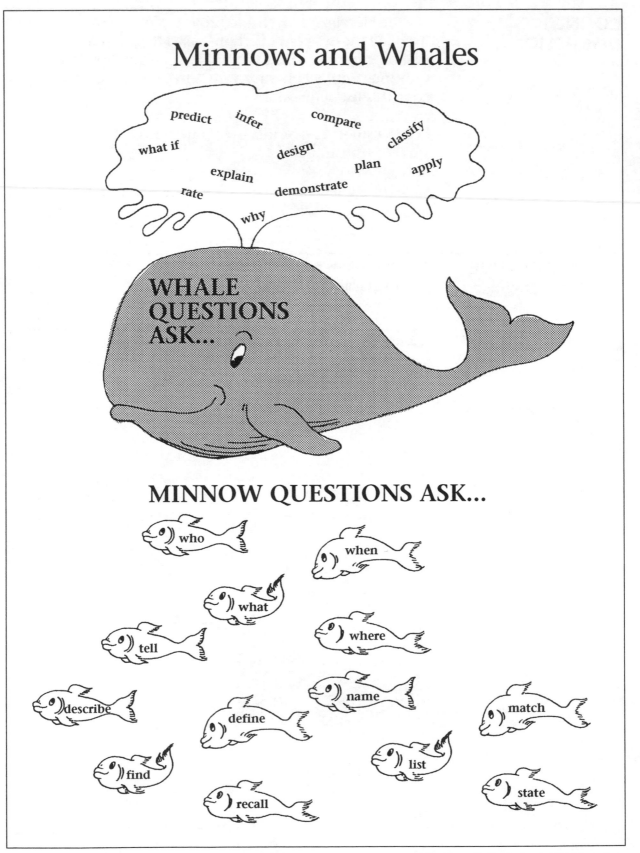

Asking Questions to Learn
What I Want to Learn

Question Level	My Goal Is...	Some Key Words to Use Are...
Gathering Knowledge (First-Story Intellect)	to learn simple facts; to collect basic information	who, what, when, where, which, name, list, identify, define, how much, how many, measure, describe
Processing Knowledge (Second-Story Intellect)	to solve problems; to use knowledge in a different context or situation	compare, contrast, explain, solve, what else, instead (of), in addition to, why, my reasons are, next, in review, in conclusion, in summary, this means
Applying Knowledge (Third-Story Intellect)	to explain my opinions; to take a position; to justify an answer; to express new ideas	devise, design, develop, I predict, I believe, in my judgment, it is my opinion (that), it seems, what if

Becoming More Focused Readers

The Prediction Guide

Chapter 4

BACKGROUND	Reading teachers tell us that students seldom read assigned science material because they find that they do not comprehend what they are reading or cannot decide what their teachers want them to learn by doing the reading. The prediction guide focuses their attention on the information that they are to learn by reading the text. The reading is not specifically assigned. The assignment is to do the prediction guide. In doing the prediction guide, students must do the expected reading.
THINKING SKILLS	Recalling, Investigating, Analyzing
FOCUS ACTIVITY	The focus activity for the reading is doing the "ME" column in the prediction guide (see pages 20 and 21). Tell students to complete the column by reading each statement and placing a "+" in front of a statement if they agree with it and a "0" if they disagree. A blackline master of the prediction guide is on page 100.
OBJECTIVES	To gather information about a topic; to learn basic vocabulary and facts.
INPUT	Explain to students that you want them to gather some information about a topic and learn its vocabulary. Tell them that the prediction guide will focus their attention on the important ideas in a reading assignment and that you will

review and add to that information as you discuss the prediction guide with them after they have completed the "AUTHOR" column.

ACTIVITY

1. Distribute a copy of the prediction guide to each student. Tell students to fill in the "ME" column. Give them a few minutes to do so.

2. Tell students which sections or pages in their textbook they must read to complete the "AUTHOR" column.

3. Tell students to complete the "AUTHOR" column by placing a "+" in front of statements that agree with the text, placing a "0" in front of statements that disagree with the text, changing "0" statements so that they agree with the text, and noting the pages in the text where the information was found.

4. Tell students that they will be given the opportunity to share their information with the class as you lead the discussion of the prediction guide. They must know that you expect them to do the reading and to be ready to participate in the discussion.

COGNITIVE DISCUSSION

Go over each item of the prediction guide. Help students organize notes about the material by outlining, mapping, or otherwise organizing information about the topic on the board or overhead projector.

Call on students to give their answers to the "AUTHOR" column. Ask them to read the original statement, tell whether the author agrees or disagrees with the statement, how they reworded "0" statements to make them agree with the text, and the page number of where they found the information. Do not worry if a student answers incorrectly—he or she may have misunderstood the text. It is often difficult for students to understand everything they read in a textbook, and the prediction guide is your way of making sure that misunderstandings are corrected early on.

METACOGNITIVE DISCUSSION

Tell the students to:

1. Write down at least two new things they learned by doing the prediction guide. Remind them that they learned something new if they disagreed with the author when they filled in the "ME" column.

2. Write down one question that they still have about the topic that you are studying.

3. Complete a logging stem that asks them to create an analogy.

   _____ is like_____ because...

   For example,
   A banana is like a washing machine because...

CLOSURE

Help students connect the day's learning with prior knowledge by telling them how it relates to some information from daily life, a unit studied earlier in the year, or material they may have learned in another class. Divide students into groups of three and ask each group to discover another connection. Ask each group to write its connection on the board. Encourage students to record the connections in their logs.

Prediction Guide: Fungi
(They are everywhere!)

Directions: Read each statement. Start with the "ME" column and place a "+" if you agree or a "0" if you disagree with the statement. Then read the textbook and decide whether or not the author agrees with the statement. Again use a "+" or a "0." Change all "0" statements so they agree with the text-book, and write down the page number of where you found the information.

ME	AUTHOR	STATEMENTS
		A fungus does not make its own food.
		Most fungi can live on things that once were alive.
		Fungi must form spores to reproduce.
		Ringworm and athlete's foot are caused by fungi.
		All mushrooms are safe for us to eat.
		Fungi always harm the living things from which they get their food.
		Lichens are made up of a fungus and another organism.
		Lichens can live on rocks.
		We have not discovered any helpful fungi.
		Yeast is a form of fungus.
		Penicillin is made by a fungus.
		Fungi get their food from plants only.
		Fungi can live on clothing.

Prediction Guide: The Moon

(Is there a man in it? Is it made of green cheese? Did the cow jump over it?)

Directions: Read each statement. Start with the "ME" column and place a "+" if you agree or a "0" if you disagree with the statement. Then read the textbook and decide whether or not the author agrees with the statement. Again use a "+" or a "0." Change all "0" statements so they agree with the text-book, and write down the page number of where you found the information.

ME	AUTHOR	STATEMENTS
		The moon has no atmosphere.
		Most of the moon's craters are very old.
		Surface temperatures on the moon do not get very high or very low.
		We see both sides of the moon from Earth.
		We would weigh just as much on the moon as we do on Earth.
		Moon rocks are light in color.
		Most of the moon's surface is covered with a fine dust.
		Shooting stars rarely hit the moon.
		The moon's gravity does not affect the Earth.
		During an eclipse, the Earth blocks sunlight from reaching the moon.

Chapter 5

Lasso a Label

The Importance of Using Precise Labels

BACKGROUND

Quantitative information must often include labels (units of measurement) to make sense. Students often find calculations difficult because they do not include labels with the numbers that they are using. Some everyday examples may help them get the point.

THINKING SKILL

Using Precise Language

FOCUS ACTIVITY

Do a think-pair-share. Ask students to identify a label that they paid attention to recently. Record the shared answers on the board or overhead.

OBJECTIVE

To include correct labels with quantitative information.

INPUT

Explain to students that when scientists talk about labeling data, they mean that correct units must accompany measurements. Measurements without labels communicate information imprecisely. In order to know the size or amount that a number describes, the number must be labeled.

ACTIVITY

Divide the class into groups of three. Each group needs a labeler, a conductor, and a scout. Each group will receive a list of ten statements that contain naked numbers (see page 26).

The labeler will be the person in the team whose clothes have the most labels on the outside. The labeler's job is to supply labels that make sense to the numbers that are naked. Give an example. What label or labels make sense in the following statement: "I will get to school on time even if I walk this morning. I only have to go four _____ ."

The conductor sits to the right of the labeler. The conductor watches the time and makes sure that everyone stays on task. The conductor also checks for agreement on the labels.

The scout's job begins when the labeler's job ends. The scout makes a copy of his or her group's labels and takes them to two other groups. He or she compares his or her group's labels with those of the other groups.

Groups will have fifteen minutes to decide on their labels and five minutes to compare them with two other teams.

Ask a student to summarize the directions for the activity. Then give each group a copy of the unlabeled numbers worksheet.

COGNITIVE DISCUSSION

Make a list of the labels that were given to the naked numbers. Call on groups at random to tell you what labels were used. More than one label may be appropriate. Discuss with the class the communications problems that nonlabeling can cause.

Tell students that they now know what you mean when you tell them to label numbers. Stress the importance of including labels whenever they record quantitative information or use it in calculations.

METACOGNITIVE DISCUSSION

Have students complete the following stem in their logs:

Labeling information is like a final step in cooking because...

Have students summarize the importance of careful labeling to complete the log entry.

CLOSURE

Ask each group to provide an example of a correctly labeled piece of information about an object in the classroom. Have meter sticks, thermometers, balances, and graduated cylinders available. Tell groups that they may choose a piece of equipment and make a measurement with it. They are then to write their correctly labeled measurement on the board. Suggest that they may make some measurements without using any of the equipment. If no group discovers that they may count objects, add your own correctly labeled count of some objects (student desks, for example) to the student list when it is complete.

Lasso A Label:
The Importance of Using Precise Labels

Directions: Fill in the label or labels that make sense.

1. I cannot carry that pile of books home! It must weigh forty_____ .

2. Wait for me! I can finish this report in two _____ .

3. We will be tired when we get to the beach. It will take us seven
    to get there.

4. It will be a big party, so I had better get five _____ of juice.

5. That rock hit the ground awfully hard! Bet it weighs one _____ .

6. I am glad that project is done! It took me three _____ to complete it!

7. There will only be two of us for dinner. One _____ of hamburger
    meat will be plenty.

8. What do you mean we ran out of hot dog buns! We bought six
    _____.

9. Let's paint the house. It looks like we will need about twelve_____
    of paint.

10. Here's a ten-dollar bill. Go to the store and get four _____ of milk.
    You will not have much change!

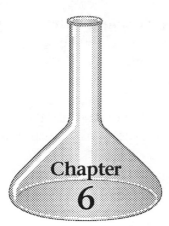

Chapter
6

And the Answer Is...
Think-Pair-Share

BACKGROUND	Many students hesitate volunteering to answer questions in the classroom. Volunteering is a high-risk response to a teacher's questions. It is much safer to wait for Johnny or Judy who always knows the right answers anyway. Think-pair-share lowers the risk by giving each student a partner with whom he or she can discuss a question and agree on the answer.
THINKING SKILL	Using think-pair-share for higher-level thinking
FOCUS ACTIVITY	Ask students "what is a synonym for *think*?" Call on students at random to share their answers. Record their answers on the board, overhead, or newsprint.
OBJECTIVES	To increase student participation in the learning process; to improve their recall, verbal communication skills, and the quality of answers.
INPUT	It is vital to explain the strategy to students before using it for the first time. They will not know what to do without some instruction.
ACTIVITY	1. Tell students to *listen* while you ask them a question. You may repeat the question to be sure that they heard it correctly. 2. Tell students to (silently and individually) *think* of an answer to the question. Tell them how long they will

have to think. Questions that involve simple answers may require seven to ten seconds of think time. More complex questions will require as much as one minute. Encourage them to jot down a few notes about their answers.

3. Next, cue students to *pair* with a neighbor and discuss their answers. During this discussion, pairs will develop a consensus answer. Pair time will vary with the complexity of the answer. Encourage pairs to record their answers as they develop with discussion.

4. Finally, ask pairs to *share* their answers with the whole class. You may ask for volunteers or call on pairs in a wraparound. List or web all of the different answers on the board, overhead, or newsprint. **Responses to student answers must be value-free if the process is to work successfully next time.**

5. You may use verbal, visual, or audio cues to move students from one step to the next. Teachers often use bells, hand signals, light signals, or the words think-pair-get-ready-to-share. Explain the cues to your students before you use the process for the first time. Remind them of the cues until they are used to them.

6. While students are thinking and pairing, observe them closely. Watch and listen. Jot down your observations.

COGNITIVE DISCUSSION

Examine the answers after they are all recorded. This is the time to modify or expand on those that need it or to eliminate any that the class (with your guidance) agrees are incorrect.

METACOGNITIVE DISCUSSION

Ask students to write a log entry about something new that they learned or a surprising point of view contributed by one of the pairs.

One new thing I learned today is...

I was surprised to hear...

Tell them to continue the log entry by analyzing their level of comfort in volunteering an answer as a member of a pair.

It was easy (difficult) for me to volunteer my answers because...

Tell them to finish the entry by describing how they will improve the next time the strategy is used.

The next time I use think-pair-share...

CLOSURE

Share some of your observations with students. Tell them what you saw and heard that was good. You may suggest improvements, but be sure that you include positive feedback. **Catch them being good at thinking!**

Kidney Bean, Jelly Bean
Making Observations

Chapter 7

BACKGROUND	Skillful observing is vital to progress in science. Students must become aware of the importance of making careful, accurate observations using all of their senses (unless tasting and touching are unsafe). Some outstanding discoveries have resulted from serendipitous observations—aspirin and aspartame are two that are frequently cited.
THINKING SKILLS	Observing, Checking for Accuracy
FOCUS ACTIVITY	Using think-pair-share, ask students to list the five senses and to describe specific information that each of the senses can give them about an object. Map their "share" answers on the board, overhead, or newsprint.
OBJECTIVES	To make accurate observations using all five senses; to check each other's observations for accuracy.
INPUT	Review the "share" map after recording all answers. Revise the map as needed.
ACTIVITY	1. Divide students into groups of three. Each group needs an **observer** who will use the five senses to make observations, a **recorder** who will write down the observations, and a **guide** who will time the activity and let the group

know when it is time to rotate roles and who will check with group members for agreement on the accuracy of observations at the end of the round.

2. The activity will take place in three initial rounds and three final rounds. Roles rotate one person to the right with each new round.

3. The objects to be observed are a kidney bean and a jelly bean. Each observer is to make as many observations about the objects as possible in one minute. The recorder and the guide may not help the observer.

4. The first-round guide is the person who lives closest to school. The first-round observer sits to the right of the guide. The first-round recorder is the third group member.

5. Be sure that all groups know who has which role for the first round.

6. Check for accuracy in understanding the instructions. Have a student repeat them.

7. Tell the first-round observers to come to your desk for three kidney beans and three jelly beans. They are to perform their observations on one bean of each kind. The other beans are for their groupmates in the succeeding rounds. Two beans of each type will be passed on to the second-round observer. The third-round observer will receive the last bean of each type. Used beans are to be discarded at the end of each round.

8. When all groups have their beans, start the initial rounds.

9. At the conclusion of the three initial rounds, signal for silence. Tell the students that they are now going to check the accuracy of their observations. The observer in each final round will receive a new kidney bean and jelly bean. The observer will then be blindfolded and will have one minute to examine the new beans and eat the one that he or she believes is the jelly bean. The observer will instantly know whether his or her observations were correct or not.

10. The roles will rotate as before. There will be three final rounds. Each group will keep score of the successful identifications—how many final-round observers correctly select the jelly bean.

11. Check for accuracy in the instructions. Tell the observers to come to your desk for a new supply of beans and a blindfold.

12. Do the final rounds.

COGNITIVE DISCUSSION	Do a wraparound in which you ask each group to tell you one unique property about kidney beans, one unique property about jelly beans, and one property that the beans have in common. Record the observations in a Venn diagram (see Chapter 11, "Frogs and Salamanders").

METACOGNITIVE DISCUSSION

Ask students to respond to the following questions in their logs:

1. How did you know you had the jelly bean?
2. What might you do differently next time?
3. What did you learn about observing with all of your senses?

Have students share their answers with others in their group.

Do a wraparound. Ask each group for its most interesting or amusing response to the questions.

CLOSURE

Tell students that you are going to analyze the effectiveness of their observation skills. Ask them to do a log entry describing their homes as seen from the street in front of the home. Ask them to check the description for accuracy when they arrive home after school and to record the results of the check in their logs.

Chapter
8

Hide in Plain Sight

Accurate Observations

BACKGROUND	Remind students of the importance of being skillful, accurate observers.
THINKING SKILLS	Observing, Checking for Accuracy
FOCUS ACTIVITY	Tell students that you are at that moment checking their powers of observation. Tell them that they have five days in which to figure out how you are doing this.
OBJECTIVE	To make accurate observations about one's surroundings.
INPUT	Tell students that their powers of observation are being tested daily in your class. Tell them to write you a note when they have discovered the test and to record their observations about the observation test in their logs. Do not tell them anything else.
ACTIVITY	Get a small but noticeable stuffed or rubber animal. Hang it someplace in your classroom where students can see it. Have it in place before you do the focus activity. Move it to a new location each day. Keep track of each location of the animal. Collect and check off notes as students figure out what you are doing.

COGNITIVE DISCUSSION

On the sixth day, announce that the test is over. Have a student tell what the test was.

Divide the class into groups of three. Have each group write or sketch the test day by day. Where was the animal each day?

METACOGNITIVE DISCUSSION

Read your record of the animal locations to the class. Tell groups to check their accuracy against your record as you read it to them.

Tell students to write a log entry analyzing the accuracy of their observations. Ask them to describe how the activity made them better observers.

Do a wraparound, asking students to tell you how the activity made them better observers. Record their answers.

CLOSURE

Give the winners (top three places—fastest to solve the test) a prize: stickers, bonus points, candy—whatever you like to use as prizes.

Part II

Catch Them
PROCESSING
Information

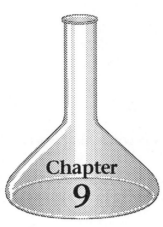

What Is Behind Door Number Two?

Mental Modeling

Chapter 9

BACKGROUND

Every scientific field involves the use of mental models to picture things that we cannot observe directly. Astronomers model the solar system and the universe; chemists model the atom; biologists model the structure of DNA. Students need to understand the processes that are involved in building these mental models.

THINKING SKILLS

Observing, Modeling

FOCUS ACTIVITY

Ask students what goes through their minds when they hear the word *model*. Do a think-pair-share. Web responses on the blackboard, overhead, or newsprint. Explain that a scientific model is a picture of something that cannot be observed directly. The picture is drawn from indirect observation and is changed as new observations are made. The model is an attempt by scientists to picture very large or very small objects.

OBJECTIVE

To develop a model of something that is hidden.

INPUT

You need to do some advance preparation for this lesson. Obtain several opaque plastic boxes—about 10" x 4" x 4"—one for each group of three students. You can pick up boxes like this very inexpensively at any hardware store or discount store with a hardware department. (I have also used cardboard boxes, but they do not work as well.) Fill the boxes as follows:

Box 1:   several nuts, bolts, washers, etc.
Box 2:   a short length of chain
Box 3:   a few handfulls of assorted buttons
Box 4:   a dozen or so clothespins
Box 5:   several empty spools from thread
Box 6:   several bottle or jar caps
Box 7:   a dozen or so pencils (old stubs without erasers are
          fine)
Box 8:   cotton balls—really pack them in tight
Box 9:   styrofoam noodles—really pack them in tight
Box 10:   newspaper—really pack it in tight

Seal the boxes with masking tape.

After the focus activity, tell students that they are going to make some observations about some object(s) that you have hidden and develop a model of the hidden object(s).

ACTIVITY

1. Divide the class into groups of three. Each group needs a recorder, model maker, and guide (to watch the time).

2. Tell the class that each group will receive a sealed box.

3. The job of each group is to make observations about the hidden contents of the box and to develop a model that pictures the possible contents of the box.

4. Group members are to rotate roles about every ninety seconds. Each group member will have a chance to perform each role.

5. A group may not open or damage the box in any way.

6. Each group will describe its model of the box contents to the rest of the class before any of the boxes are opened.

7. Be sure that students understand the instructions. Ask a student, selected at random, to repeat them.

8. Begin the activity.

COGNITIVE DISCUSSION

Have each group describe its model of the contents of its box. Record the descriptions.

If at all possible, have the boxes X-rayed. Before opening the boxes, show the X-rays to the class and ask them to comment on the accuracy of the models based on what they see in the X-rays. Some of the boxes may still hide their contents. Cotton balls (Box 8), for example, do not show up on an X-ray.

Open the boxes. Let students react as they see how closely their models describe the contents of each box.

METACOGNITIVE DISCUSSION

Have each group answer these questions about the activity:

1. What were we asked to do?
2. How well were we able to do it?
3. What else could we be permitted to do to develop more accurate models?
4. What did we learn about the process of developing mental pictures of things that cannot be directly observed?

CLOSURE

Have each group read its answer to the last question aloud. Emphasize the difficulty that scientists have in trying to develop models of things that are very large, very small, or very far away.

What a Bright Idea
Becoming Better Listeners

BACKGROUND	Good ideas and discoveries often come from brainstorming sessions in which large numbers of ideas are generated. These ideas must be offered in a safe-risk setting—put downs are not allowed. In the real world, ideas are evaluated and kept or rejected only after the initial brainstorming has occurred.
THINKING SKILLS	Active Listening, Generating Ideas
FOCUS ACTIVITY	Tell students that before Columbus sailed, he was told, "The earth is flat! You will fall off the edge!" Ask volunteers to contribute other famous historical put downs.
OBJECTIVES	To practice generating ideas in a safe-risk environment; to practice responding to others' ideas in a positive way.
INPUT	Remind students of the DOVE guidlines (see the blackline master on page 94).
ACTIVITY	1. Divide the class into groups of three.
	2. Tell each group to brainstorm a list of ten things that give off light and to wait for further instructions. Tell them to be sure that the group has a recorder to write down the list.

3. As groups finish their lists, give each group a randomly chosen number that corresponds to one of the items on the list. Have the recorder circle that item.

4. Each group now needs an idea person and a responder. The recorder will keep his or her role for the time being.

5. The idea person, sitting to the recorder's right, is to suggest an improvement to the light-generating item that was circled.

6. The responder is to say to the idea person, "That improvement is a good idea because...."

7. The recorder is to write down the improvement and the response.

8. The roles then rotate one person to the right. The activity proceeds until each person has had two turns at being the idea person.

9. The group is then to do a graphic that shows their improved light-giving device. Each member of the group must be able to explain the graphic.

10. When all of the graphics are finished, have each group present its graphic to the class.

11. Decorate the room with the graphics.

COGNITIVE DISCUSSION

Ask students to write a log entry in which they describe the requirements that must be met for an object to produce light.

METACOGNITIVE DISCUSSION

Have each group answer these questions:

1. How did this activity promote our creativity?

2. How did the brainstorming guidelines help us do our job well?

3. When could we use this process again?

CLOSURE

Ask students to write a log entry describing a place where or a time when they could use their improved light-giving device.

Frogs and Salamanders

The Venn Diagram

Chapter 11

BACKGROUND

The Venn diagram is an old visual tool for comparing and contrasting that has its roots in philosophy. When new math sprang onto the scene, using Venn diagrams was very popular in all content areas. That popularity faded for a while, but use of the Venn diagram has revived because it is a very effective way to organize information.

THINKING SKILLS

Comparing, Contrasting

FOCUS ACTIVITY

Ask students to give you some synonyms for the word *characteristics* (or *attributes*). Do a think-pair-share. Record shared answers on the board, overhead, or newsprint.

Hold up a textbook and a notebook. Ask students to find similarities and differences in the two objects. Suggest that they write down their answers in their logs.

Call on students at random. Ask each student to give you one way in which the books are similar and one way in which they are different. Record their answers.

OBJECTIVE

To compare and contrast objects using a Venn diagram to organize the information.

INPUT

Find another teacher who will be your partner. (If you have trouble finding a teacher who can join your class, ask for a student volunteer.) Draw the Venn circles on the blackboard. Label the circles.

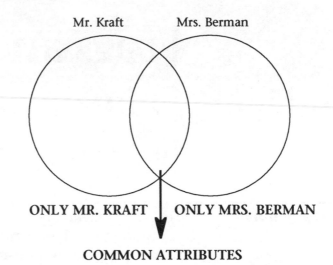

Mr. Kraft   Mrs. Berman

ONLY MR. KRAFT   ONLY MRS. BERMAN

COMMON ATTRIBUTES

Ask one student, called on at random, to name one unique characteristic of your partner (Mr. Kraft). Ask another student to name one of your own unique attributes. Ask a third student to name an attribute that you and your colleague share. Record their answers in the appropriate sections of the Venn diagram. Continue for a few more rounds. Students will quickly catch on and have fun learning to Venn by using attributes of their teachers.

ACTIVITY

1. Divide students into groups of three. Give each group a sheet of newsprint, a pizza pan, and three different colored markers.

2. Explain to students that they are to use the pizza pans to draw circles for a Venn diagram. It will help them see what is going on if each circle is a different color.

3. Give each group one copy of the "Frogs and Salamanders" reading (see next page) or assign a similar section in your science textbook.

FROGS AND SALAMANDERS

Frogs and salamanders are amphibians. All amphibians are cold-blooded—their body temperatures adjust to the temperatures of their surroundings. Amphibians must lay their eggs in water because the eggs will dry out on land and because the hatchlings breathe with gills, just like fish! Adult amphibians breathe with lungs, so they can live on land.

Frogs have four legs. The two front legs are small and the two back legs are large and powerful. The large back legs allow frogs to jump long distances. Frogs have long, sticky tongues that they use to catch the insects they eat. Frogs have no tails. Adult frogs have no gills.

Salamanders have four legs of about equal size. They also have long tails. Some kinds of salamanders keep their gills and live in water for their whole lives.

4. Tell students that their job is to organize the information from the reading using a Venn diagram. Supervise the drawing and labeling of the circles.

5. Give students a reasonable time limit. Ten minutes is plenty for the sample reading.

6. Post the results.

COGNITIVE DISCUSSION

Have students do a log entry in which they summarize what they learned about the two objects without refering to the assigned reading or the Venn diagram. Then have them compare their summaries with the information in the Venn diagram produced by their group and correct the log entries as needed.

METACOGNITIVE DISCUSSION

Ask students to summarize how they did the task. First, have them write log entries; then lead a class discussion. Point out differences in thinking styles that are reflected in different approaches to the task.

Ask students to continue the log entry by recording how their teammates helped them with the task.

CLOSURE   Ask students if they can think of other pairs of objects that they can compare and contrast using a Venn diagram. Have them write their ideas in their logs. Then do a wraparound, asking randomly selected students for ideas. Record their answers on the board, overhead, or newsprint.

Chapter
12

The Planets Organized

Using a Fishbone

BACKGROUND	A fishbone graphic organizer looks like its name. It can be used in a number of ways. In this activity, a fishbone will be used to organize information about the planets in our solar system.
THINKING SKILLS	Organizing Information, Analyzing for Attributes
FOCUS ACTIVITY	Hold up a pen, a pencil, a piece of chalk, and a marker. Ask students to start thinking about attributes of the four objects. Draw a fishbone graphic organizer on the blackboard, overhead, or newsprint. Label the fishbone as shown.

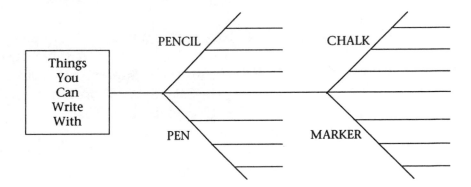

Explain to students that the angled bones are used for main categories and the horizontal bones are used for details.

Fill in the fishbone with attributes of the writing tools. Call on students for ideas.

OBJECTIVE

To organize attributes of the planets in our solar system using a fishbone graphic organizer.

INPUT

Remind students of the meaning of *attributes* or *characteristics*. If you saved your list of synonyms from the focus activity in Chapter 11, "Frogs and Salamanders," this would be a good time to pull it out and share it with the class.

Tell students that they will be organizing attributes of planets in the solar system using a fishbone. Ask them how many main angled bones they will need. Be sure that they know how to set up the fishbone—the head is the title (The Solar System) and the angled bones are labeled with the main topics (names of the planets).

ACTIVITY

1. Divide the students into groups of three.

2. Each group will need a recorder, checker, and reader.

3. Give each group a reading passage that summarizes the attributes of each of the planets in the solar system. Most earth science books contain a section that does this in just a few pages.

4. Give each group a sheet of newsprint, a straightedge, and assorted markers. Have them draw and label the outline of the fishbone. Supervise this closely. The head is labeled "The Solar System" and there is a main (angled) bone for each planet.

5. Give students time to fill in details about each planet on the fishbone.

6. Post the results.

COGNITIVE DISCUSSION

Have students write a log entry that summarizes the information that they organized about the planets. They should write without consulting the reading or the fishbone. Completed log entries are then checked against the fishbone and corrected as needed.

METACOGNITIVE DISCUSSION

Ask students to log their responses to these questions:

1. What were we asked to do?
2. What did we do well?
3. Summarize the process that was used and think about how you would do it differently next time.
4. What did you learn?

Have group members share their individual log entries with one another.

CLOSURE

Ask groups to brainstorm other situations in which they can use a fishbone to organize information. Call on groups to share their ideas with the rest of the class. Record the ideas. Suggest that this technique can be especially helpful to organize information during review of a topic before a test.

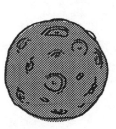

That Is My Pet Matrix

One Way to Use a Matrix

BACKGROUND	The ability to list or describe the attributes of items is crucial to good critical thinking. Only by recognizing the attributes of something can we distinguish that item from others and recognize it when we encounter it again.
THINKING SKILLS	Analyzing for Attributes, Organizing Information
FOCUS ACTIVITY	Do a think-pair-share in which you ask students to name a synonym for *classify*. Record the shared responses on the blackboard, overhead, or newsprint.
OBJECTIVE	To identify the attributes that can be used to identify items.
INPUT	Remind students that they may use all of their senses to determine the attributes of items. Suggest that there may be times when they choose not to use one of the senses. Draw the following matrix on the board or overhead.

Attributes						
Pets	size	skin covering	warm- or cold-blooded	legs (?)	other appen-dages	food
dog						
cat						
fish						
bird						
other						
other						

Ask students to suggest other attributes that may be useful in identifying a kind of pet and in distinguishing one kind of pet from another: bedding, shelter, teeth, and odor are some possibilities.

ACTIVITY

1. Divide students into groups of three. Each group needs a recorder, checker, and scout. The scout may leave the group to get materials—newsprint and markers—and to trade information about attributes with other groups. The recorder will draw the matrix on the newsprint and fill in group answers. The checker will poll group members to be sure that agreement has been reached before an answer is recorded in the matrix.

2. Each group will fill in the matrix completely. Emphasize that some discussion may be necessary before an answer is recorded for a type of pet. Stress that such discussion results in the sharing of unique information that each member brings to the activity and that group members must focus on answers that are complete and accurate. Remind students to criticize or critique ideas, not people. Each individual is to be treated with respect.

3. Ask a student to repeat the instructions.

4. Give the groups thirty minutes to set up and fill in a matrix on a large sheet of newsprint.

| **COGNITIVE DISCUSSION** | Post and discuss the matrices. Ask each group to describe a lively discussion it had about one of the attributes for one type of pet. |

| **METACOGNITIVE DISCUSSION** | Ask groups to decide how they could use the matrix in another class—English, math, social studies, physical education. Call on each group to share one answer with the rest of the class. Record the answers. If time permits, do another wrap-around. |

| **CLOSURE** | Have students write a log entry in which they define *attribute* and *classify*. |

Scavenger Hunt

Looking for Attributes

BACKGROUND	An object may be much more than it seems to be. Students can sharpen their imaginations and prediction skills by looking at objects in new ways.
THINKING SKILLS	Analyzing Attributes, Predicting
FOCUS ACTIVITY	Hold up a pen, a baster, and a cardboard tube from a roll of paper towels or toilet paper. Do a think-pair-share by asking students to name an attribute that all three have in common. Record shared answers on the board or overhead.
OBJECTIVE	To find attributes that can be used to group objects in common or uncommon ways.
INPUT	Draw a fishbone graphic organizer on the board or overhead. Remind students that the angled bones are labeled with the names of major categories and the horizontal bones are used for details. In this activity, the major categories are the attributes that are used to form groups of objects and the details are the objects that fit each attribute. For example, the pen, baster, and cardboard tube are all objects that are hollow, or objects that roll, or whatever other attributes pairs of students name in the focus activity.

| ACTIVITY | The day before doing this activity, tell students that their homework for the next class is to bring four small objects from home. All four must fit easily into one sandwich bag. |

1. Divide the class into groups of three. Each group needs a recorder, conductor, and sorter. The activity will have three rounds. Roles rotate one person to the right with each round.

2. The person in the group who brought the smallest object will be the first-round sorter. The job of the sorter is to pool all of the objects brought by group members and then to sort out groups of two, three, or four objects that have a common attribute. The sorter is to name the attribute that he or she used in putting together each group of objects. The sorter is to find as many groups of two, three, or four objects as he or she can in one minute.

3. The recorder is the person to the right of the sorter. The recorder writes each attribute named by the sorter on an angled fishbone and records the names of the objects with a given attribute on the horizontal bones.

4. The conductor watches the clock and tells the group when it is time for the roles to rotate.

5. The conductor and the recorder may not help the sorter.

6. Give each group a sheet of newsprint and markers or a copy of a fishbone graphic organizer. (You may use the blackline master on page 102.)

7. Ask a member of the class to repeat the instructions. Remind students that they may look at objects in uncommon ways when determining attributes.

8. Help the conductors watch the one-minute time limit as groups do the activity.

| COGNITIVE DISCUSSION | Draw a fishbone graphic organizer on the blackboard. Ask each group for its most interesting attribute and the objects that fit that attribute. Record the answers on the board. Post the group fishbones. |

METACOGNITIVE DISCUSSION

Have each group answer the questions below. The final recorder will write the consensus answers and all group members will sign the product.

1. What were we asked to do?
2. What did we do well?
3. What would we do differently next time?
4. What did we learn about looking at objects for uncommon attributes?

CLOSURE

Have each individual write a log entry:

This activity was fun and helped me stretch my imagination because...

Part III

Catch Them
ANALYZING and APPLYING
Information

Chapter
15

Cook's Choice

Lateral Thinking

BACKGROUND	Lateral thinking, invented by Dr. Edward de Bono, forces students to look at ideas and objects in new and different ways. It can be used to improve understanding or to develop new ways of solving problems. However it is used, lateral thinking generates exciting discussions in the classroom.
THINKING SKILL	Generating Ideas
FOCUS ACTIVITY	Do a think-pair-share. Ask students, "What is one way in which digesting food is like cooking food?" Record shared answers on the blackboard, overhead, or newsprint.
OBJECTIVE	To generate ideas through lateral thinking that will improve understanding of the way in which the digestive system works.
INPUT	Ask students to recall the DOVE guidelines. Call on students at random to tell you what each of the letters stands for. Ask them why it is important to use the DOVE guidelines when they are brainstorming together.

ACTIVITY

1. Divide the class into groups of three.

2. Tell the groups that their job will be to design a graphic that shows the human digestive and excretory systems as a series of interconnected kitchen utensils.

3. Have each group brainstorm a list of utensils.

4. Each utensil is to be used for an appropriate purpose. For instance, students would not use a baster to cut or shred food or use a blender to separate a mixture of foods.

5. A utensil may be used for a nontraditional purpose. For example, students may choose to use a rolling pin to crush food or a sifter to separate large from small pieces of food.

6. The parts of the digestive and excretory systems are to be shown in order. Food is taken in at the mouth and solid waste passes out from the large intestine. Dissolved wastes are excreted using a separate pathway. Utensils must be connected in the same order as the organs that they represent.

7. The utensils are to be labeled with the name of the part of the digestive and excretory systems that each represents.

8. The graphic is to be done on newsprint.

9. Set a time limit for completion of the graphic. Thirty minutes is a good idea.

10. Check to see if there are any questions. Ask a student, chosen at random, to repeat the instructions.

11. The assigned roles within each group are: the conductor, who keeps an eye on the time and keeps the group on task; the encourager, who maintains the confidence of the group; and the gopher, who gets the newsprint and markers and who returns the markers to their proper place. Group members may decide among themselves who will do the drawing and coloring. (A group may decide, for example, to have one student do the drawing lightly in pencil and the others color in the sketches while the artist moves on to a new portion of the graphic.)

12. Have each group present its completed graphic to the class.

COGNITIVE DISCUSSION	Ask students to write a log entry identifying the most important role of each of the major organs in the digestive and excretory systems.
METACOGNITIVE DISCUSSION	Ask students to continue the log entry by identifying one way in which the activity helped them better understand the function of one of the major organs and how the systems fit together. Have students share their log entries with members of their groups.
CLOSURE	Display completed graphics in the classroom. Celebrate the success of the activity with a round of applause or another type of celebration of your choice.

Chapter
16

Dear Uncle Chester
An Individual Writing Activity

BACKGROUND

When students can explain a concept or phenomenon clearly in their own words, they demonstrate their personal ownership of the item. Asking students to write their explanations encourages them to focus their thoughts in order to express them as clearly as possible. Their successful completion of the writing assignment demonstrates basic understanding of the concept.

THINKING SKILL

Explaining

FOCUS ACTIVITY

Simultaneously drop a raw egg and a hard-boiled egg onto a hard surface (a pizza pan works nicely). Show students the results of dropping the eggs. Ask them to explain what you did and why the eggs behaved the way they did. Challenge them to explain the egg drop so clearly that someone who did not witness it would understand what was done and what happened just by reading their explanation. Tell them that they need to describe what happened step by step. Let them volunteer their ideas. Record the ideas on the board, revising as you go.

OBJECTIVE

To clearly explain a concept or phenomenon.

INPUT

Describe the importance of good explanations to the students. Do a think-pair-share. Ask students to think of a time when a poor explanation led them to an incorrect conclusion. Call on students at random to share their partners' examples of poor explanations with the class.

ACTIVITY

1. This is an individual writing activity.

2. Give each student a copy of the following paragraph. Have each student read the paragraph silently.

> Your assignment is to write a letter to your Uncle Chester in which you explain (*any concept or lab activity that the class has studied or done recently—this is an effective alternative to the traditional lab report*). Uncle Chester is very bright, but his formal education ended when he graduated from high school. He is very interested in you and what you are doing in school. He especially likes to hear about what you have learned or done recently in science class. Remember that you are explaining, so write the letter in your own words. Your goal is to help Uncle Chester understand (*the concept or lab activity*) just as well as he would if he were a member of this class. Make the letter as long as you think it needs to be so Uncle Chester knows what is going on. (Paper lengths will vary due to students' handwriting.)

3. Tell students what they are to write about.

4. Tell students that the rough drafts of the letters are due the following day.

5. The next day divide students into groups of three.

6. Tell students that they are going to proofread and critique each other's letters.

7. Tell them that after they have formed their circles, each student is to pass his or her letter to the student on his or her right.

8. That student is to read the letter, mark spelling and punctuation errors, and write marginal notes at points where they do not understand what is being said or believe that more needs to be said.

9. Proofreaders will have ten minutes to read the letters and critique them.

10. The original proofreader will pass the letter to the student on his or her right. The new proofreader will have five minutes to make additional comments. The second proofreader is really backing up the work done by the first.

11. The second proofreader will return the letter to its author. Each student will write a second draft of the letter as homework for the following day. The new draft should address the corrections and other comments made by the proofreaders.

12. Tell students that you will collect and grade the second draft of the letter.

13. Return graded letters to students as quickly as possible.

COGNITIVE DISCUSSION	Do a think-pair-share. Ask students what they learned about inelastic collisions, that is, collisions in which the objects do not bounce off of each other. Call on pairs to share their answers. Record the answers.
METACOGNITIVE DISCUSSION	Ask students what they found easiest (hardest) about writing the letter. Call on students at random to share their answers with the class. Ask students if they visualized Uncle Chester as they wrote to him. Brainstorm a picture of Uncle Chester.
CLOSURE	While students are working on their letters, write one general reply from Uncle Chester. When graded letters are returned, read Uncle Chester's reply to the class.

Chapter 17

Elements, Compounds, and Mixtures

A Jigsaw

BACKGROUND	Jigsaw is a way of dividing responsibility for teaching and learning among members of a group. Each member of the group is assigned a specific portion of the material to master. That person then may join other experts on the same portion of the material to decide how to teach the material and to practice those teaching strategies. Members of a team then rejoin each other for the actual teaching/learning. Jigsaw is most effective if this initial round of teaching and learning is followed by additional review of the material.
THINKING SKILLS	Explaining (Teaching), Active Listening
FOCUS ACTIVITY	Do a think-pair-share. Ask students to tell you: A) what famous detective is often (mis)quoted: "It is elementary, my dear Watson!", B) what you call it when a bone is broken in more than one place, and C) what you call the contents of a package that contains all of the ingredients that are needed to make a cake (except, perhaps, the liquid or eggs or shortening). Record the answer to each question on the board before proceeding to the next question.
OBJECTIVE	To be able to classify something as an element, a compound, or a mixture given its name or a description of one or more of its properties.

INPUT

Give each student a 3" x 5" card that has *element, compound,* or *mixture* written on it. Then ask students to pick up the passages that correspond to their cards (see pages 104-106 for blackline masters). Give them these passages at the end of class on the first day of the lesson and ask them to read their passages and be ready to discuss them with other experts on the same passage the next day.

ELEMENT: Elements are pure substances that contain only one kind of atom. Two or more of these atoms may bond together to form molecules. Elements are the simplest substances known. Only about one hundred of them have been found in nature on earth. Elements cannot be chemically changed into other substances. Elements are homogeneous—all parts of an element look and act like all other parts of the same element. Some common elements are oxygen, hydrogen, copper, iron, gold, aluminum, and carbon.

COMPOUND: Compounds are pure substances whose molecules are always identical. Atoms of two or more elements bond together to make molecules of compounds. Water molecules, for example, always contain two hydrogen atoms bonded to one oxygen atom. Silica molecules always contain one silicon atom bonded to two oxygen atoms. In a molecule of table salt, one sodium atom is bonded to one chlorine atom to produce sodium chloride. Compounds can be chemically broken apart into the elements that formed them. Compounds are homogeneous— all parts of a compound look and act like all other parts of the same compound. Millions of compounds are known. Some common compounds are salt, sugar, water, carbon dioxide, baking soda, and sulfuric acid.

> **MIXTURE:** Mixtures contain two or more elements or compounds that are not chemically combined. The composition of a mixture may vary—there are lots of different ways to make salt water, for example. The percents of the two substances in the mixture will not always be the same. Mixtures may be separated physically or chemically. To separate a salt water mixture, you could just let the water evaporate out of the mixture. Mixtures are not always this easy to separate. It may be very tricky to separate a mixture of salt and sugar. Mixtures may be homogeneous—all parts of the mixture may look and act the same. Milk and mayonnaise are homogeneous mixtures. Mixtures may also be heterogeneous—different parts of the mixture may look and act differently. Asphalt and wood are heterogeneous mixtures. Millions of mixtures are known. There are more natural mixtures than elements or compounds. Some common mixtures are milk, wood, vinegar, concrete, brick, dirt, dishwater, and a pail of garbage.

ACTIVITY

1. Hand out the element, compound, and mixture cards and have students pick up the reading passages toward the end of class. Tell students to read their individual passages before the next class meeting.

2. At the beginning of the next class period, get expert groups together. Form groups of three. This means that you will have three or four groups for each category. Have each expert group plan a teaching strategy and have each expert in each group do a graphic that he or she will use as part of the teaching process. Check out progress and understanding in the expert groups. It is vital that you, the teacher, monitor the expert groups to correct misunderstandings before the teaching round begins. When an expert group finishes its work, tell members to thank each other and return to their seats to wait for further instructions.

3. You may want to place a time limit of ten minutes on the expert group portion of this lesson. This will encourage students to stay on task and to get the job done in a reasonable amount of time.

4. When all expert groups are finished, divide the class into groups of three. Now each group should contain one student from element, one from compound, and one from mixture.

5. Have each expert teach his or her portion of the material to the rest of the group. Tell students that their job as learners is to listen actively, ask questions, and request clarification of ideas that they do not understand. Their job as teachers is to explain their portion of the material, using the visual they created as a teaching tool and to answer questions and clarify information for the members of their group.

6. Have students do the next round—teaching and learning in turn. Again it is vital that you, the teacher, monitor the groups and correct any misunderstandings that you observe.

7. Encourage students to thank each other at the end of this round.

COGNITIVE DISCUSSION

Have students write a log entry in which they record the best, most complete definitions of element, compound, and mixture that they can recall without referring to the visual or the reading.

METACOGNITIVE DISCUSSION

Ask students to think and jot down individual answers to be shared with their groups:

1. Which was harder, teaching or listening?
2. What was the most effective teaching strategy used by a member of the group?
3. How could the teaching strategies be improved?
4. Did you take any notes when you were a listener?
5. Does taking notes help you as a learner?

CLOSURE

Call on students at random to contribute ideas from their cognitive log entries to make a class summary of elements, compounds, and mixtures. Record their answers in an outline or a mind map on the board. Fill in any glaring omissions. Thank students for a job well done.

Elements, Compounds, and Mixtures

Follow-Up for Guided Practice

BACKGROUND	Although proponents of cooperative learning view jigsaw as an excellent way to promote interdependence among members of a group, critics insist that jigsaw can be one of the least effective ways for students to learn new information or concepts. The critics may be correct if teachers who use a jigsaw overlook one key component of all learning—follow-up of initial activities with guided practice and drill.
THINKING SKILLS	Identifying Ideas, Analyzing for Attributes
FOCUS ACTIVITY	The initial jigsaw provides the focus activity for the follow-up.
OBJECTIVES	To be able to apply the definitions of elements, compounds, and mixtures to new examples; to use previously learned information in a new activity.
INPUT	Give each student a copy of the follow-up activity. Rotate the focus. The student who initially learned and taught information about elements is to look for compounds in the follow-up. Compounds is to focus on mixtures. Mixtures is to look for elements. Assign initial work on the follow-up as homework.

Chapter 18

Elements, Compounds, and Mixtures
Applying What We Have Learned

Directions: Decide which of the following is an example of _____.

(an element, a compound, or a mixture)

Circle your choices (answers).

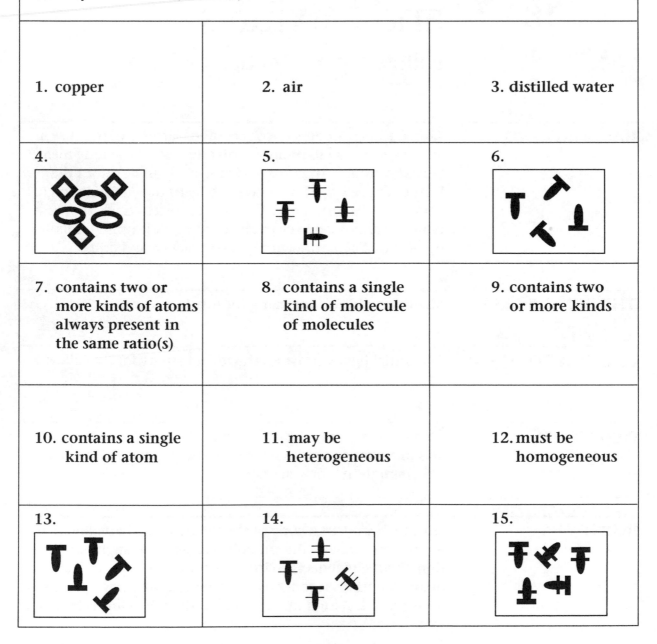

1. copper	2. air	3. distilled water
4.	5.	6.
7. contains two or more kinds of atoms always present in the same ratio(s)	8. contains a single kind of molecule of molecules	9. contains two or more kinds
10. contains a single kind of atom	11. may be heterogeneous	12. must be homogeneous
13.	14.	15.

ACTIVITY	1. Hand out the follow-up activity worksheet. Be sure that students understand that the focus is to rotate—and how to rotate. Be sure that each student knows what to look for as he or she does the follow-up as homework.
	2. Before groups begin the next day, tell them that each person is to tell the group which items in the follow-up activity he or she identified as belonging to his or her category and why that item fits the category. If members of a group disagree about how to classify an item, they must discuss their reasons for wanting to classify it in different ways and reach consensus about the best way to categorize or classify the item before they move on to another.
	3. When the group has finished classifying the items on the follow-up, they are to sign one completed copy of the follow-up sheet and turn it in. Their signatures signify that they all agree to accept the grade earned by the paper that is turned in.
	4. Call on a student to repeat the instructions.
	5. Have groups circle and complete the activity.
COGNITIVE DISCUSSION	After all groups have turned in their papers, go over the answers for the follow-up. Have a copy of the activity on the overhead. Call on groups at random to tell how they classified an item and why they so classified it. Discuss the answers, especially if there is disagreement (from you or another group) with the initial answer. Be sure that the class knows the right answers and why those answers are correct before they leave the room.
METACOGNITIVE DISCUSSION	Have students write a log entry in which they compare and contrast the attributes of elements, compounds, and mixtures. They will rely on their memories as they write. Have them continue the log entry by writing one unanswered question that they still have about the topic.

CLOSURE

Call on students at random to share their questions with the class. Make a list of the questions on the overhead or on newsprint. Save the questions and refer to them as you progress with your study of the topic. Ask students to answer their own questions when class activities have provided them with the information that they need to develop those answers.

Home on the Range
Just Is Not the Same

Using a Storyboard

BACKGROUND	Good thinkers are skilled in visualizing and predicting. The more clearly one can see, the better one can understand a problem or situation. It was Leo Szilard's ability to see a neutron penetrating and splitting a nucleus that led to the successful splitting of the atom. His visualization of the process not only enabled him to convince others that splitting the atom was possible, but allowed scientists to predict which kinds of atoms should be easiest to split. The more skilled students become at visualizing and predicting, the more effectively they will think.
THINKING SKILLS	Visualizing, Predicting
FOCUS ACTIVITY	Ask students to close their eyes and picture themselves getting ready for school. Tell them to see the scene in as much detail as possible. Have each student share his or her visualization with a partner.
OBJECTIVE	To practice the skills of visualization and prediction.
INPUT	Give students a copy of the following scenario or show it on the overhead projector (see page 107 for a blackline master).

> Clint Clifford is a modern-day cattle rancher in southern Wyoming. He runs his cattle on several thousand acres of grassland and forest. Clint loves ranching, except for one problem. It is really hard dealing with problems caused by several kinds of dinosaurs. You see, dinosaurs never became extinct. Clint must deal with dinosaur-related problems each day.

Draw a storyboard that shows one day in Clint's life.

Tell students that a storyboard is like a comic strip. It tells a story in a series of pictures. The pictures may be accompanied by text. Storyboards are used to plan television commercials and programs and are used in plotting movies.

ACTIVITY

1. Assign a rough draft of the storyboard as homework. Tell students that a good storyboard has more pictures than text, uses color lavishly, and may be funny.

2. The next day divide the class into groups of three.

3. Each group is to do a storyboard on a large sheet of newsprint.

4. Remind students to use the DOVE guidelines as they brainstorm their group stories.

5. Ask for questions. Then have groups do their storyboards.

COGNITIVE DISCUSSION

Have students write a log entry in which they discuss all of the facts about dinosaurs that they needed to recall in doing their stories. Call on students at random to list responses.

METACOGNITIVE DISCUSSION

Have groups discuss how they resolved differences in individual stories to obtain the group story, what they feel they did well in producing the storyboard, and what they would do differently if they were to do it over.

Have each student do a log entry discussing the visualizing and predicting process. Ask students to write in some detail about how they approached the assignment. Ask them to reconstruct their thinking step by step.

CLOSURE

Have each group present its storyboard to the class. Display the storyboards in the classroom.

Chapter 20

Making Sense of What We Know

Mapping

BACKGROUND	A mind map is a diagram that is used to organize information and show relationships that exist between different pieces of the information. Maps can be used in place of outlines. Maps are particularly appealing to nonlinear thinkers.
THINKING SKILLS	Analyzing, Summarizing, Visualizing
FOCUS ACTIVITY	Any information-gathering activity is a good focus activity for mapping.
OBJECTIVE	To organize and analyze information.
INPUT	Teach students the rules for mapping. It is particularly effective to map the rules on the board, overhead, or newsprint rather than just listing them.

RULES FOR MAPPING

1. Do maps on plain white paper.

2. Start maps at the center of the paper. The title and a picture illustrating the title are in the center, not at the top of the paper.

3. PRINT ALL TEXT IN UPPERCASE LETTERS.

4. There are different formats that may be used in mapping.

    a. A thick line leading from the center (title) carries each main idea. Supporting details are carried on thin lines hanging from the thick ones.

    b. A circle that is connected to the center (title) carries a main idea. Small circles attached to a large one carry supporting details.

5. Lines or circles and text for each main idea and its details are all done in the same color. Different main ideas are done in different colors.

6. Use pictures to illustrate text.

7. Delete incorrect information by crossing it out.

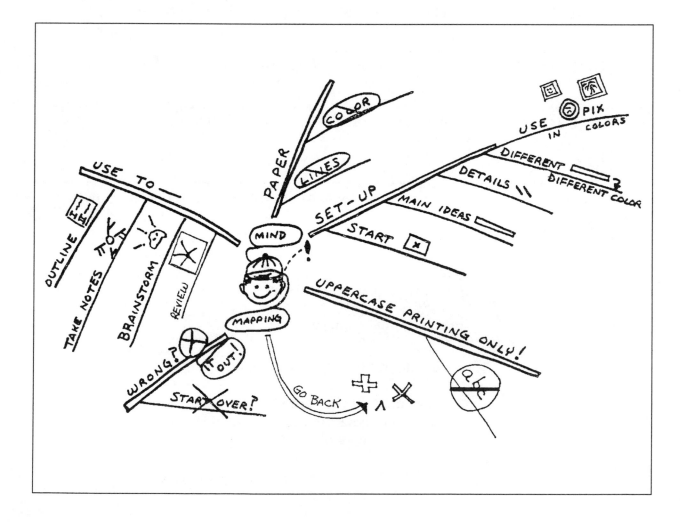

ACTIVITY	1. Assign a rough draft of an individual map to be done as homework.
	2. The final draft may be an individual assignment or a group assignment.
	3. If the final draft is a group assignment, it is very effective to have groups do the map on large sheets of newsprint and present them to the class.
	4. Groups of three or four are a good size for a mapping assignment. The group is large enough to provide its members with a variety of ideas but not so large that there is not enough work to keep all members involved.
	There is a sample map on copper at the end of this chapter (see next page).
COGNITIVE DISCUSSION	Call on groups or individuals at random to present their maps to the rest of the class.
METACOGNITIVE DISCUSSION	Ask students to write a log entry in which they identify the following:
	One way that I can use mapping in another class is...
	One good idea that I got from another student's map is...
	One way that I will improve my mapping technique the next time is...
CLOSURE	Display the group or individual maps in the classroom.

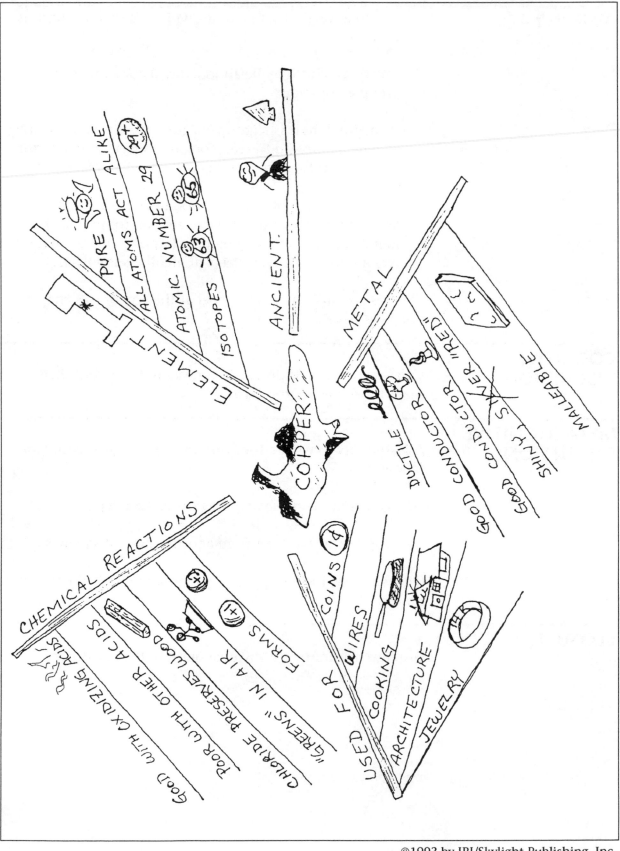

Molecules in Motion

Right-Angle Thinking

Chapter 21

BACKGROUND	Right-angle thinking forces students to associate ideas and to generalize or draw conclusions based on acquired information. Using the graphic organizer helps them see their thinking in action.
THINKING SKILLS	Associating Ideas, Drawing Conclusions
FOCUS ACTIVITY	Do the following demonstration: place a small volume of sand in one balloon, a small volume of water in a second, and a small volume of air in a third. Ask students to jot down a few notes about the behavior of each balloon. Next, pour a small volume of sand into the center of a large (one liter) beaker, a small volume of water in the center of a second beaker, and a small volume of air into the center of a third. Ask students to jot down a few notes about the behavior of each sample of matter. Finally, fill one large syringe (without the needle!) with sand, fill a second with water, and a third with air. Push on the plunger of each syringe after filling it— try to compress each sample. Ask students to jot down a few notes about the compressibility of each sample.
OBJECTIVE	To use right-angle thinking to associate compressibility and shape of solids, liquids, and gases with motion of molecules and distances between molecules.

INPUT   Discuss the notes that students wrote during the observation.
                            Call on students at random to share their observations with
                            the rest of the class (ask each student who is called on to
                            share one specific observation). Use these observations to
                            guide students to the following ideas: solids are not compress-
                            ible and do not rely on their containers for their shapes;
                            liquids are not compressible but do rely on their containers
                            for their shapes; gases are very compressible and rely on their
                            containers for their shapes.

ACTIVITY   1. Divide students into groups of three.

                            2. Tell students that their task is to complete a right-angle
                                thinking diagram (see next page) for each of the states of
                                matter: solid, liquid, and gas.

                            3. The horizontal arm of each diagram is used to describe
                                shape-dependence and compressibility of one of the states
                                of matter.

                            4. The vertical arm of the diagram is used to describe dis-
                                tances between molecules, their freedom (or lack of it) to
                                move from place to place in that state of matter, and
                                other possible types of molecular motion.

                            5. Each member of the group is to complete one of the three
                                diagrams and explain his or her conclusions about mo-
                                lecular motion and spacing to the other members of the
                                group.

                            6. Ask for questions. Call on a student selected at random to
                                repeat the instructions.

                            7. Set a time limit for the activity.

                            8. Ask each group to have a scout pick up three copies of the
                                right-angle thinking diagram.

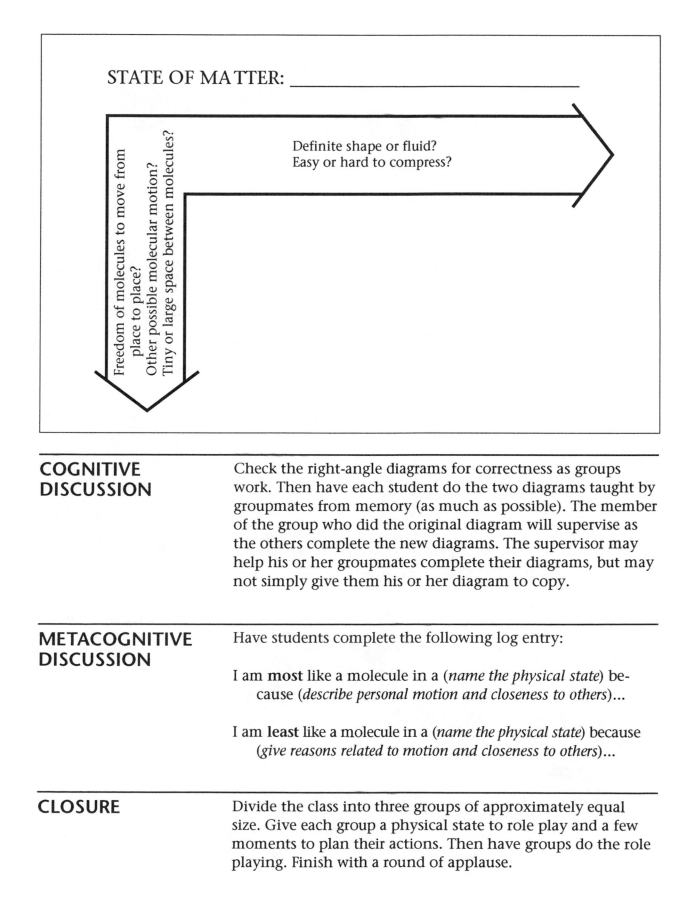

STATE OF MATTER: _____

Freedom of molecules to move from place to place?
Other possible molecular motion?
Tiny or large space between molecules?

Definite shape or fluid?
Easy or hard to compress?

COGNITIVE DISCUSSION

Check the right-angle diagrams for correctness as groups work. Then have each student do the two diagrams taught by groupmates from memory (as much as possible). The member of the group who did the original diagram will supervise as the others complete the new diagrams. The supervisor may help his or her groupmates complete their diagrams, but may not simply give them his or her diagram to copy.

METACOGNITIVE DISCUSSION

Have students complete the following log entry:

I am **most** like a molecule in a (*name the physical state*) because (*describe personal motion and closeness to others*)...

I am **least** like a molecule in a (*name the physical state*) because (*give reasons related to motion and closeness to others*)...

CLOSURE

Divide the class into three groups of approximately equal size. Give each group a physical state to role play and a few moments to plan their actions. Then have groups do the role playing. Finish with a round of applause.

Bibliography

American Chemical Society. (1988). *ChemCom: Chemistry in the community*. Dubuque, IA: Kendall/Hunt Publishing Company.

Aronson, E. (1978). *The jigsaw classroom*. Beverly Hills, CA: Sage Publications.

Bellanca, J. (1990). *Keep them thinking: Level III*. Palatine, IL: IRI/Skylight Publishing, Inc.

Bellanca, J., & Fogarty, R. (1986). *Catch them thinking: A handbook of classroom strategies*. Palatine, IL: IRI/Skylight Publishing, Inc.

Bellanca, J., & Fogarty, R. (1991). *Blueprints for thinking in the cooperative classroom*. Palatine, IL: IRI/Skylight Publishing, Inc.

Brinkerhoff, R.F. (1992). *One minute readings: Issues in science, technology and society*. Menlo Park, CA: The Alternative Publishing Group (Addison Wesley Publishing Co.).

Christensen, J. (1991). *Global science: Energy, resources, environment*. Dubuque, IA: Kendall/Hunt Publishing Company.

Fogarty, R., & Bellanca, J. (1987). *Patterns for thinking: Patterns for transfer*. Palatine, IL: IRI/Skylight Publishing, Inc.

Fogarty, R., & Haack, J. (1986). *The thinking log.* Palatine, IL: IRI/Skylight Publishing, Inc.

Fogarty, R., & Opeka, K. (1988). *Start them thinking: A handbook of classroom strategies for the early years.* Palatine, IL: IRI/Skylight Publishing, Inc.

Gotimer, K.K. (Executive Editor). (1993). *Science, technology, and society.* (text series). Columbus, OH: Globe Book Co., Simon & Schuster.

Gridley, C., & Roberts, R. (1992). *Asking better classroom questions.* Portland, ME: J. Weston Walch.

Holmes, O.W. (1916). *The poet at the breakfast table.* Boston, MA: Houghton Mifflin.

Jenkins, D.C. (1991). *Amusing problems in physics.* Portland, ME: J. Weston Walch.

Johnson, D.W., Johnson, R., & Holubec, E. (1988). *Advanced cooperative learning.* Edina, MN: Interaction Book Company.

Johnson, D.W., Johnson, R., & Holubec, E. (1988). *Cooperation in the classroom.* (revised edition). Edina, MN: Interaction Book Company.

Johnson, D.W., Johnson, R., & Holubec, E. (1987). *Structuring cooperative learning: The 1987 handbook of lesson plans for teachers.* Edina, MN: Interaction Book Company.

Johnson, D.W., Johnson, R., & Holubec, E. (1986). *Circles of learning: Cooperation in the classroom* (revised edition). Edina, MN: Interaction Book Company.

Winkler, A., Bernstein, L., Schachter, M., & Wolfe, S. (1989). *Concepts and challenges in science.* Columbus, OH: Globe Book Co., Simon & Schuster.

Masters

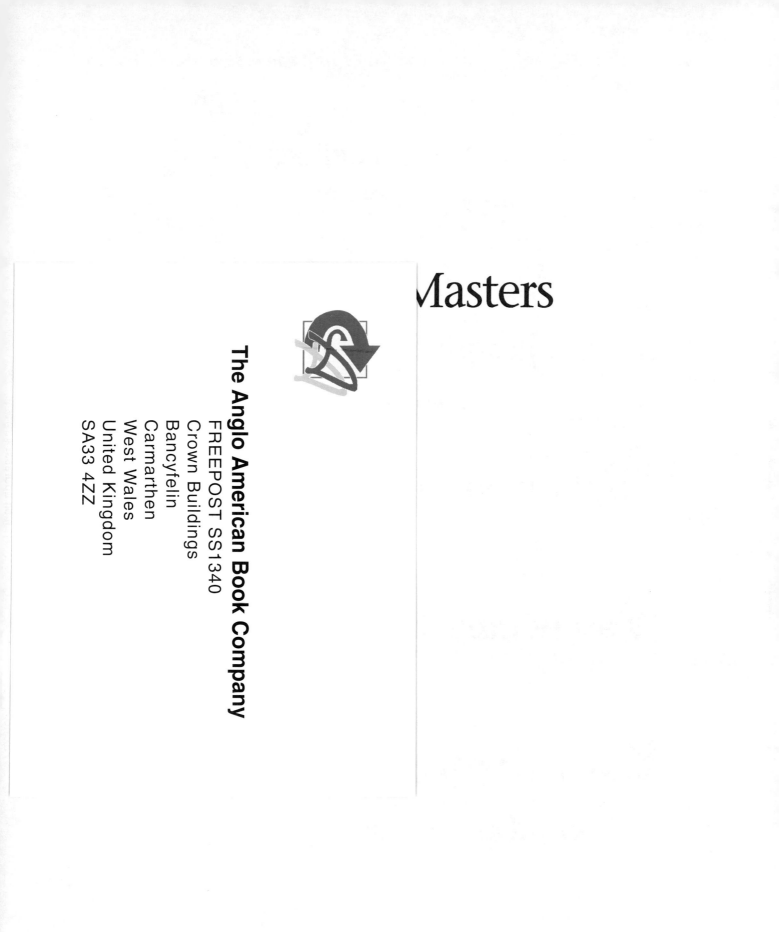

The Anglo American Book Company
FREEPOST SS1340
Crown Buildings
Bancyfelin
Carmarthen
West Wales
United Kingdom
SA33 4ZZ

DOVE Guidelines

Defer judgment; anything goes

Opt for original; different ideas

Vast number is needed

Expand by piggybacking
on other's ideas

Mrs. Potter's Questions

1. What were you supposed to do?

2. What did you do well?

3. What would you do differently next time?

4. Do you need any help?

People Search

Directions: Find someone who can give you an answer for each of the items below. A classmate may sign for only one item, so you will need ten different signatures. Sign only if you know the answer or be prepared to accept the consequences!

My signature means that I...

1. _____

_____

2. _____

_____

3. _____

_____

4. _____

_____

5. _____

_____

6. _____

_____

7. _____

_____

8. _____

_____

9. _____

_____

10. _____

_____

KNL

K	N	L
(What do we Know?)	(What do we Need to know?)	(What have we Learned?)

Minnows and Whales

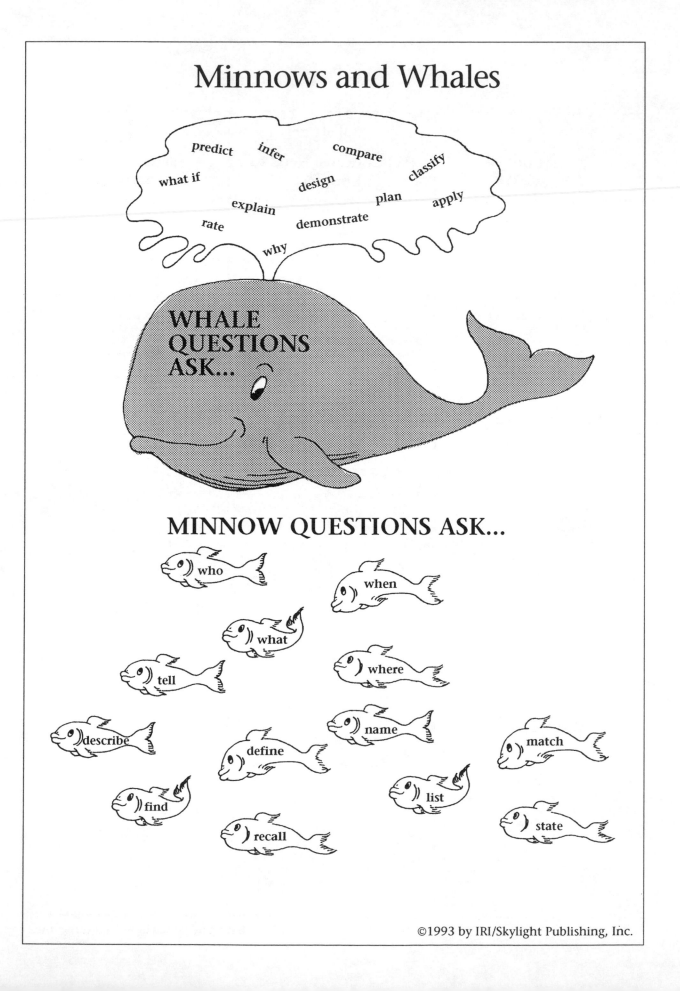

Asking Questions to Learn What I Want to Learn

Question Level	My Goal Is...	Some Key Words to Use Are...
Gathering Knowledge (First-Story Intellect)	to learn simple facts; to collect basic information	who, what, when, where, which, name, list, identify, define, how much, how many, measure, describe
Processing Knowledge (Second-Story Intellect)	to solve problems; to use knowledge in a different context or situation	compare, contrast, explain, solve, what else, instead (of), in addition to, why, my reasons are, next, in review, in conclusion, in summary, this means
Applying Knowledge (Third-Story Intellect)	to explain my opinions; to take a position; to justify an answer; to express new ideas	devise, design, develop, I predict, I believe, in my judgment, it is my opinion (that), it seems, what if

Prediction Guide: _____

Directions: Read each statement. Start with the "ME" column and place a "+" if you agree or a "0" if you disagree with the statement. Then read the textbook and decide whether or not the author agrees with the statement. Again use "+" or a "0." Change all "0" statements so they agree with the textbook, and write down the page number of where you found the information.

ME	AUTHOR	STATEMENTS

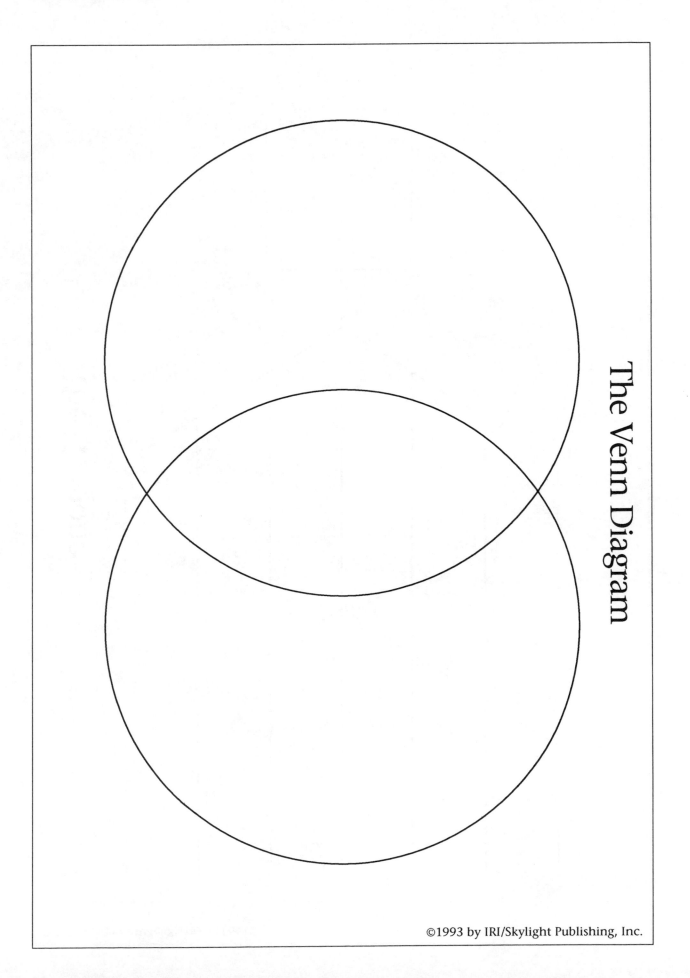

The Venn Diagram

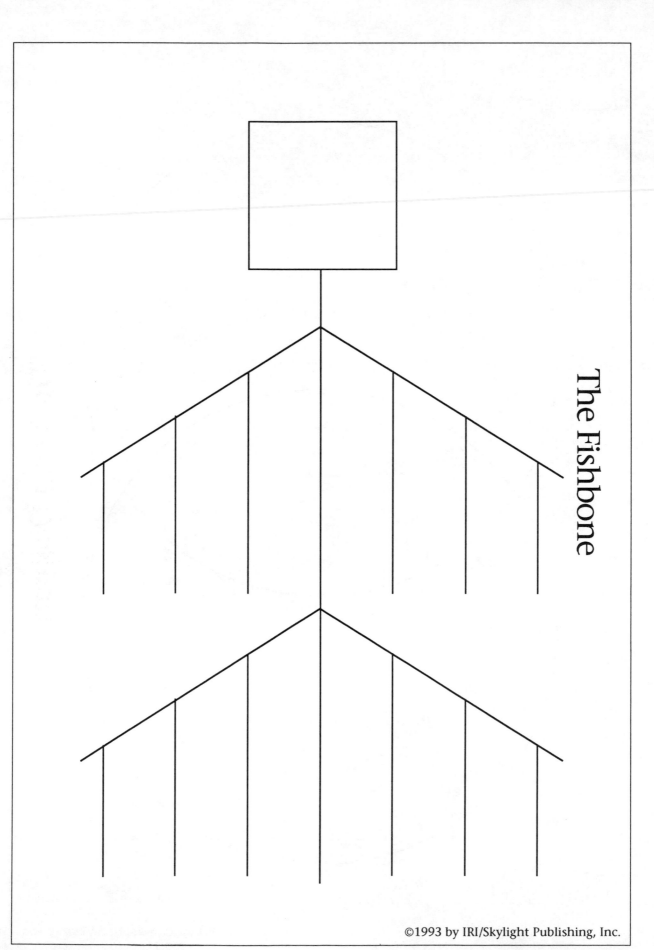

The Fishbone

Matrix

Subjects	Attributes					

Element

Elements are pure substances that contain only one kind of atom. Two or more of these atoms may bond together to form molecules. Elements are the simplest substances known. Only about one hundred of them have been found in nature on earth. Elements cannot be chemically changed into other substances. Elements are homogeneous—all parts of an element look and act like all other parts of the same element. Some common elements are oxygen, hydrogen, copper, iron, gold, aluminum, and carbon.

Compound

Compounds are pure substances whose molecules are always identical. Atoms of two or more elements bond together to make molecules of compounds. Water molecules, for example, always contain two hydrogen atoms bonded to one oxygen atom. Silica molecules always contain one silicon atom bonded to two oxygen atoms. In a molecule of table salt, one sodium atom is bonded to one chlorine atom to produce sodium chloride. Compounds can be chemically broken apart into the elements that formed them. Compounds are homogeneous—all parts of a compound look and act like all other parts of the same compound. Millions of compounds are known. Some common compounds are salt, sugar, water, carbon dioxide, baking soda, and sulfuric acid.

Mixture

Mixtures contain two or more elements or compounds that are not chemically combined. The composition of a mixture may vary—there are lots of different ways to make salt water, for example. The percents of the two substances in the mixture will not always be the same. Mixtures may be separated physically or chemically. To separate a salt water mixture, you could just let the water evaporate out of the mixture. Mixtures are not always this easy to separate. It may be very tricky to separate a mixture of salt and sugar. Mixtures may be homogeneous—all parts of the mixture may look and act the same. Milk and mayonnaise are homogeneous mixtures. Mixtures may also be heterogeneous—different parts of the mixture may look and act differently. Asphalt and wood are heterogeneous mixtures. Millions of mixtures are known. There are more natural mixtures than elements or compounds. Some common mixtures are milk, wood, vinegar, concrete, brick, dirt, dishwater, and a pail of garbage.

Storyboard

Clint Clifford is a modern-day cattle rancher in southern Wyoming. He runs his cattle on several thousand acres of grassland and forest. Clint loves ranching, except for one problem. It is really hard dealing with problems caused by several kinds of dinosaurs. You see, dinosaurs never became extinct. Clint must deal with dinosaur-related problems each day. Draw a storyboard that shows one day in Clint's life.

Right-Angle Thinking

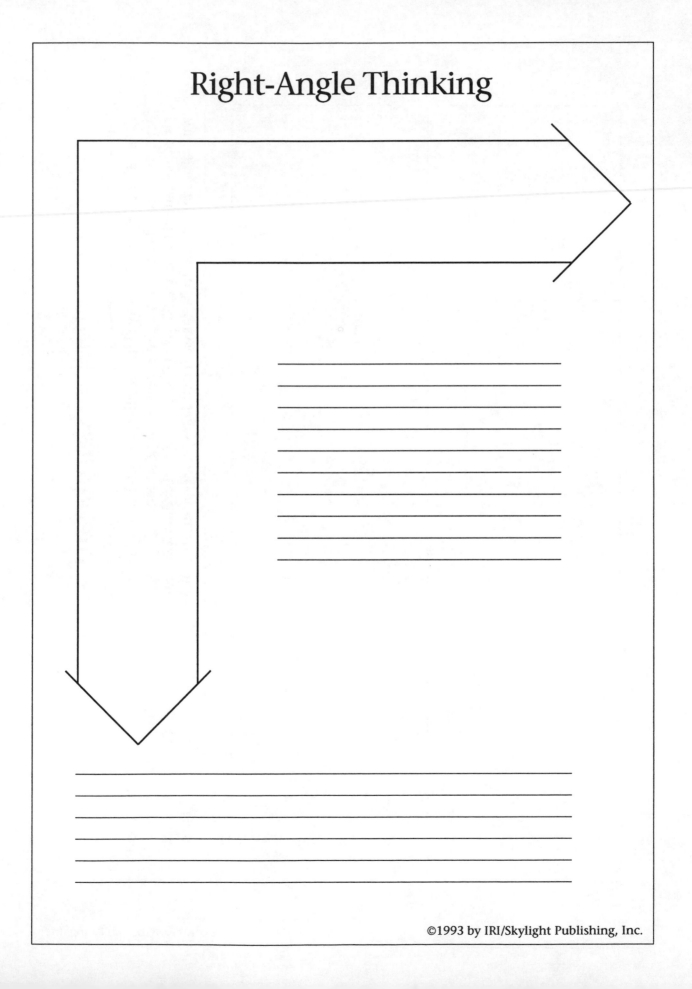

NOTES

NOTES